Searching for Truth

I am very grateful to the Reverend Shelagh Brown and the Bible Reading Fellowship for the invitation to write this Lent book. I thank my secretary, Mrs Josephine Brown, for her unfailing skill and helpfulness in typing drafts of the manuscript, and my wife, Ruth, for her help in correcting the proofs. The scriptural quotations are all taken from the New Revised Standard Version.

John Polkinghorne
Queens' College
Cambridge

SEARCHING FOR TRUTH

A scientist looks at the Bible

John Polkinghorne

The Bible Reading Fellowship
OPENING THE BIBLE

Published by
The Bible Reading Fellowship
Peter's Way, Sandy Lane West
Oxford, OX4 5HG
England
ISBN 0 7459 3298 3
Albatross Books Pty Ltd
PO Box 320, Sutherland
NSW 2232, Australia
ISBN 0 7324 1559 4

First edition 1996
10 9 8 7 6 5 4 3 2 1 0

Acknowledgments
Unless otherwise stated, scripture quotations are
taken from the New Revised Standard Version of
the Bible copyright © 1989 by the Division of
Christian Education of the National Council of the
Churches of Christ in the USA.

A catalogue record for this book is
available from the British Library

Printed and bound in Great Britain
by Biddles Ltd, Guildford & Kings Lynn

CONTENTS

FOREWORD

In the late 1980s, when I first heard about John Polkinghorne's work, I was at once intrigued by the idea that science and religion could be discussed together with fruitful results. I had already become interested in the interface between Christianity and psychology, both of which shed light on the soul, and now I saw that the interface between Christianity and physics could be equally mind-expanding, since both explored God's creation.

In the summer of 1990 I finally bought Dr Polkinghorne's acclaimed trilogy—*One World*, *Science and Creation* and *Science and Providence*—and read the volumes in rapid succession. Despite the fact that I was scientifically illiterate I found them not only comprehensible and stimulating but even, I would go so far as to say, a revelation. My parents' generation had been brought up alongside the myth that science had destroyed religion. I now saw that in the modern world this erroneous belief could no longer be intellectually sustained; I realized not only that science and religion were different facets of one truth, but that each could complement the other in the quest for knowledge and wisdom. It then seemed to me of vital importance that a post should be founded at the highest academic level to research and teach in this crucial area.

At the end of that year the *Sunday Times* asked me to nominate three books which I had recently enjoyed reading, and I included Dr Polkinghorne's *Science and Creation*. Shortly afterwards I received a letter from him, thanking me for including his work on my list, and I wrote back to ask him if he ever preached in London. No sooner had I dropped his letter in the postbox than I had a telephone call inviting me to a special lecture which was to be given at the City of London church, St Lawrence Jewry, and followed by a dinner at the Mercers' Hall. Having accepted this invitation I asked who was lecturing and was told: 'The Reverend Dr John Polkinghorne'.

We finally met in the church just before the lecture began, but that wasn't the end of the story, because the big surprise of the evening was still to come: at dinner I found I had been placed next to him. Our conversation made me keener than ever to found a university post devoted to the science/religion field, and matters came to a head when I was taken to dine at Queens' College Cambridge on a guest night. There, waiting to receive me, was none other than the President of the College—John Polkinghorne! It was at the end of the evening when he came to sit next to me that I finally took the plunge and told him I wanted to found a chair or lectureship in his special subject. His reply was: 'What a coincidence—the Regius Professor and I have just submitted a paper to the University to say how important it is that such a post be created.'

Some months later the Starbridge Lectureship in Theology and Natural Science was established.

I relate this story not just to record what happened, by the grace of God, when my path crossed with John Polkinghorne's, but also to testify to his power and skill as a Christian communicator. He has the rare gift of being able to express complicated matters simply, and with the aid of his pellucid, utterly readable style he presents in *Searching for Truth* his deeply spiritual meditations in a way which his readers will find unusually satisfying. Here is both a wise priest writing as a gifted scientist and a wise scientist writing as a gifted priest.

'People are sometimes surprised that I'm both a physicist and a priest,' he writes. 'They think there's something odd, or maybe even dishonest in the combination. Their surprise arises because they don't realize that truth matters just as much in religion as it does in science. There is an odd view around that faith is a matter of shutting one's eyes, gritting one's teeth and believing impossible things because some unquestionable authority tells you that you have to. Not at all! The leap of faith is a leap into the light and not into the dark. It involves commitment to what we understand in order that we may learn and understand more...'

This book, *Searching for Truth*, gives us the chance to follow up our own 'leap into the light' by journeying farther along the spiritual way. It is a journey into the truth about reality, and I can personally vouch for the fact that John Polkinghorne is one of the most inspiring and clear-sighted of guides.

Susan Howatch

INTRODUCTION

The Bible

Modern science began when people realized that if you are to find the truth you can't just sit around and think about it. You have to go out and see what has actually happened. The ancient Greeks were very clever thinkers but they hadn't cottoned on to the need for observation and experiment. They thought it was obvious that a heavy object fell faster than a light one, so they never bothered to check up whether this was in fact the case. When Galileo did so, he found that both fell at the same rate (after allowing for the effect of air resistance, which is what makes a feather flutter slowly down).

The search for religious truth is similar. If we want to know what God is like we shall have to find out what he has done and how he has made himself known. The Bible is the most important record of religious experience that we have to help us in that search for truth. The section that Christians call the Old Testament is concerned with how God encountered some wandering shepherd chiefs, like Abraham; how God brought their descendants out of slavery in Egypt; how God was involved with the history of the people of Israel, both in judgment and in deliverance. If we read the Bible with some regularity, we shall get to know a lot about Israelite history—the triumphs under King David and King Solomon; the splitting into two Kingdoms, North and South, which were subsequently defeated and deported by the Assyrians and the Babylonians, respectively; the return of a band of exiles to rebuild Jerusalem and its temple. In all these events the prophets saw the hand of God at work through history. At the same time that the prophets were declaring, 'Thus says the Lord', the Wisdom writers, in books like Job, were reflecting on how strange the world is and wrestling with the problem of suffering, and the writers of the Psalms were expressing, with unparalleled honesty, their feelings of both trust and desolation.

These are such familiar themes to those of us who read the Bible that we find it hard to remember what an insignificant nation Israel actually was. Outside of the Old Testament, it has left very little mark on the historical records. The nations which really seemed to matter in the ancient Middle East were those based in the fertile river valleys of the Nile and of the Tigris and Euphrates. Israel and Judah were just small countries caught in between these giant empires, like Hungary caught between Germany and Russia in World War II. There is only one reason why we have heard of the Israelites: because they came to know God in a special way which is still important for us today.

In the New Testament, we read of how God has acted to make himself known in a new and clearer way. The Gospels tell us about the life and death and resurrection of Jesus, whilst the other writings (such as Paul's letters)— many of which are earlier than the Gospels—tell us how the first Christians were overwhelmed by the new life they had found in Christ. Here is recorded the experience which led the Church to the central and profound Christian idea of the incarnation: that God has lived a human life, and shared in human suffering and death, and triumphed over it, in the historical person of Jesus Christ. We shall have a lot to say and think about this astonishing and exciting claim in connection with the Bible readings that follow.

It is very important to recognize that the Bible is not a book but a library. It contains writings of many different kinds: prose and poetry, history and story, laws, letters and prophecies. Part of our respect for scripture must be to figure out exactly what it is we are reading. It is a terrible mistake to read poetry as if it were prose. When Robert Burns says that his love is like a red, red rose, we know that he doesn't mean that his girlfriend has green leaves and prickles! When we read the first chapter of Genesis, we know that we are not reading a divinely-guaranteed textbook of scientific cosmology in the modern manner. It is something different and, in fact, even more interesting, as we shall see.

The Bible was written by people. I do not doubt that they were divinely inspired in what they wrote, but the Bible was not divinely dictated. Our Islamic friends believe that the Qur'an was written in heaven in classical Arabic and then infallibly communicated to Muhammad by an angel. Christians have never thought of the Bible in that way. It was written at many different times, and the writers had to express the eternal truth which they had discovered in the thought and style of their own age. One of the problems we have in reading scripture is to sort out what is true for all time and what is just an expression of the culture of the writer's own day. Slavery is an accepted fact in the Bible, as it was in the whole of the ancient world. Yet, when Christians like William Wilberforce began in the late eighteenth century their great campaign for the abolition of slavery, surely they were truer to the spirit of scripture than were their opponents who pointed to the acceptance of slavery in its pages. Today we recognize that there is much that was culturally conditioned in ancient views about the status of women and we are more likely to look to Paul for guidance when he makes his great assertion that in Christ there is 'no longer male and female'

(Galatians 3:28), than to look to the patriarchal narratives of early Israel.

So far, I have been writing about the Bible as evidence, as the record of spiritual experience from which we can learn about God's ways with humanity. When we read scripture in this way we are necessarily to some extent subjecting it to our judgment. We have to decide whether we are reading a historical account or a story (for example, Jonah), whether what is said reflects God's will or human custom (for example, Paul's remarks about women covering their heads during worship). I think we need to read the Bible in this way, but we certainly need also to read it in other ways as well. In particular, we are not only to judge it but we must allow it to judge us. An indispensable manner of reading scripture is the slow, meditative, reflective way in which perhaps just a few words are allowed to dissolve in our minds, enter our hearts and become part of us. It is an aspect of the inspired nature of scripture that it can be read in this way and that it has a transforming and strengthening power when we encounter its truth in this accepting fashion. When, day by day, you go over the readings that follow, I hope you will allow space for this to happen. As you work through a passage, a word or phrase or sentence may speak particularly to you. I cannot tell what that will be; it will be different for different people. Train yourself to recognize this and then allow yourself the time to dwell on it. Keep the word or verse in your mind; it may recur to you during the day. This is one of the ways in which God speaks to us individually. It may very well be that at first sight you will not know what he is saying. But by allowing the words to dissolve and enter your being, something will be happening that the Spirit will use for your spiritual growth.

A scientist's approach

Whatever it is that we do in life, the experiences we have will colour our thoughts and mould our ways of thinking. I have spent thirty years of my life working as a theoretical physicist, trying to use mathematics to understand some of the beautiful patterns and order of the physical world. For good or ill (and no doubt it is a mixture of both) this affects how I think about all sorts of things. The way I like to characterize my habits of thought is to say that I am a 'bottom-up' thinker.

What I mean by that is that I like to start with the phenomena, with things that have happened, and then try to build up an explanation and an understanding from there. 'Start with particular cases and only then try to go on to understand what's happening in general' is my motto. If you're a 'top-down' thinker, you like to go the other way: start with some grand general ideas and use them to explain particular events.

Bottom-up thinking is natural for a scientist for two reasons. One is that we are looking for ideas which have reasons backing them up; these reasons will lie in the evidence we consider, the events that motivate our belief. The second point is that we have learnt that the world is full of surprises. That means it is very hard to guess beforehand what the right general ideas will turn out to be. Only experience can tell us that. In fact, this element of surprise is one of the things that makes scientific research worthwhile and exciting. You never know what you'll find round the next corner.

Let me give you just one example of these scientific surprises. Every day of my working life as a theoretical physicist I used the ideas of quantum mechanics. This theory describes how things behave on a very small scale, the size of atoms or even smaller. It turns out that the behaviour of the very small is totally different from the way we experience the world on the feet-and-inches scale of everyday life. We seem to live in a world which is reliable and picturable. We know where things are and what they are doing. All this changes when you get down to the level of atoms. Take an electron, one of the constituents of an atom. If you know where it is, you cannot know what it is doing; if you know what it is doing, you cannot know where it is! (This is called Heisenberg's uncertainty principle.) The quantum world is fuzzy and unpicturable. We cannot imagine in everyday terms what it is like. Nevertheless we can *understand* it, using mathematics and the special set of quantum ideas which we have learnt about from a bottom-up approach to atomic phenomena.

No one could have guessed beforehand that matter would behave in this very odd way when looked at subatomically. In fact it took many extremely clever people twenty-five years to figure out what was happening. If you want to understand nature, you have to let the physical world tell you what it's like. You have to start at the bottom, with actual behaviour, and work your way up to an adequate theory.

Now, if the physical world is so full of surprises, it would be strange if God didn't also exceed our expectations in quite unexpected ways. Commonsense thinking by itself won't be adequate to tell us what he's like. We'll have to try to find out from how he has actually made himself known. That's why I was keen in the preceding section to think of the Bible as a source of evidence about how God has acted in history and, above all, in Jesus Christ. It's a natural strategy for a bottom-up thinker to pursue.

You'll see, in fact, that I find there's a lot in common between the way I search for truth in science and the way I search for truth in religion. People are sometimes surprised that I'm both a physicist and a priest. They think there's something odd, or maybe even dishonest, in the combination. Their surprise arises because they don't realize that truth matters quite as much in religion as it does in science. There is an odd view around that faith is a matter of shutting one's eyes, gritting one's teeth and believing impossible things because some unquestionable authority tells you that you have to. Not at all! The leap of faith is a leap into the light and not into the dark. It involves commitment to what we understand *in order that we may learn and understand more*. You have to do that in science. You have to trust that the physical world makes sense and that your present theory gives you some sort of idea of what it's like, if you are to make progress and gain more understanding and a better theory. You'll never see anything if you don't stick your neck out a bit! You have to do the same in the religious quest for truth. We shall never have God neatly packaged up. He will always exceed our expectations and prove himself to be a God of surprises. There is always more to learn.

There is one important difference, however, between scientific belief and religious belief. The latter is much more demanding and more dangerous. I believe passionately in quantum theory, but the belief doesn't threaten to change my life in any significant way. I cannot believe in God, however, without knowing that I must be obedient to his will for me as it becomes known to me. God is not there just to satisfy my intellectual curiosity; he is there to be honoured and respected and loved as my Creator and Saviour. Beware! Let me utter a theological health warning or, rather, promise: 'Reading the Bible can change your life.'

Lent and Easter
Although this is a Lent Book, and so concerned with a time when Christians particularly think about the Lord's passion, we can never separate the death of Christ from

16

the resurrection of Christ. We need to hold the two together in our hearts and minds. That is not because the good news of the resurrection is there to cancel out the bad news of the crucifixion and make everything nice and happy in the end. What is going on is much more profound that that. The death of Christ is part of reality and of his sharing our humanity to the uttermost. The one certainty of our lives is the inevitability of our deaths. Jesus' way to his Easter vindication lay inescapably through the darkness and death of Good Friday.

The passion is real but it is not the whole of reality, for the empty tomb is part of reality also. We are destined to die, but our ultimate destiny, in the eternally faithful purposes of God, is that we shall live in Christ.

For that reason, I have chosen within Lent to speak also of Easter. The readings for each Sunday are mostly selected to remind us of the central Christian truth: 'Jesus lives!'

STARTING LENT

SIN

P s a l m   5 1 : 1 – 5

Have mercy on me, O God,
  according to your steadfast love;
according to your abundant mercy
  blot out my transgressions.
Wash me thoroughly from my iniquity,
  and cleanse me from my sin.
For I know my transgressions,
  and my sin is ever before me.
Against you, you alone, have I sinned,
  and done what is evil in your sight,
so that you are justified in your sentence
  and blameless when you pass judgment.
Indeed, I was born guilty,
  a sinner when my mother conceived me.

A great American theologian of this century, Reinhold Niebuhr, once said that there was only one Christian doctrine that you could easily check on experimentally— the doctrine of human sinfulness. You only have to look around you, or within your own heart, to see that it is true. I don't mean that we are all incredibly evil. It would be an unhealthy kind of self-dramatization for most of us to think of ourselves in that sort of way. But there is something wrong with human life and we share in it. There is a twistedness which means that hopes are tarnished and good intentions so often get frustrated and come to nothing. A country's liberator becomes its next tyrant; the innocence of youth is changed into the dusty compromises of middle-age. And even the innocence of youth can be exaggerated. We all know how cruel quite young children can be to someone who is a little bit different and doesn't quite fit in with the ways of the gang.

Where does this twistedness come from? Is it just the effect of 'selfish genes' forcing us to fight our corner in the battle for life and survival? The Christian diagnosis is much more profound than that. It tells us that we are not made to go it alone. We are not the masters of our souls and the captains of our fate. We are creatures who will only find fulness of life if it is lived in communion with our Creator. The root of sin is an alienation from God, arising because we have made the mistake of believing that we are self-sufficient. That is not a popular message to proclaim at this present time when there is a great deal of emphasis on individualism, on doing your own thing. Yet I believe it is a true message and there could be no better way of beginning Lent than to acknowledge our need of God.

This understanding of sin as a chosen separation from God explains why the Psalmist says to God, 'Against you, you alone, have I sinned'. Traditional Jewish thinking attributed Psalm 51 to King David's repentance after he had been so cleverly convinced of his sinfulness by the story that the prophet Nathan had told him (2 Samuel 12:1–13). David had had Uriah the Hittite murdered so that he could take his wife, Bathsheba, whom David had seduced into adultery. You might have thought that Uriah and Bathsheba were the injured parties. Although David had done them a terrible wrong, it all originated from his determination to follow his own way without regard for God.

When the Psalmist says that he was 'a sinner when my mother conceived me', I do not at all think this means that sex is in itself sinful or degraded. Nor does it at all mean that little babies are in themselves condemned. Past generations have made some very bad mistakes by thinking in these ways. Yet it is true that through our conception and birth we joined a human race which has lost its way and a society which will seek to instil into us the false ideal of 'doing it my way'.

The first step in regaining health is to know that one is ill and in need of healing. Acknowledgment of our sinfulness is not a morbid act of self-destructiveness but the way in which we can begin to find the forgiveness and grace offered to us by the God of 'steadfast love' and 'abundant mercy'.

PRAYER

Almighty and everlasting God, you hate nothing that you have made and forgive the sins of all those who are penitent. Create and make in us new and contrite hearts, that, lamenting our sins and acknowledging our wretchedness, we may receive from you, the God of all mercy, perfect forgiveness and peace; through Jesus Christ our Lord.

ASB, Collect for Ash Wednesday

LOOKING AT LIFE

Genesis 3:16–19

To the woman [God] said, 'I will greatly increase your pangs in childbearing; in pain you shall bring forth children, yet your desire shall be for your husband, and he shall rule over you.' And to the man he said, 'Because you have listened to the voice of your wife, and have eaten of the tree about which I commanded you, "You shall not eat of it," cursed is the ground because of you; in toil you shall eat of it all the days of your life; thorns and thistles it shall bring forth for you; and you shall eat the plants of the field. By the sweat of your face you shall eat bread until you return to the ground, for out of it you were taken; you are dust, and to dust you shall return.'

There was death in the world long before there were human beings. The dinosaurs died out about 70 million years ago, whilst our first ape-man ancestors only appeared a few million years ago; thorns and thistles have been around for a long time. We cannot interpret the powerful and ancient story in Genesis 3, as some of our Christian predecessors used to do, as a story of how a world that was a paradise got spoiled because of a disastrous mistake made by the first man and the first woman. Nevertheless, it is still a story with a meaning for us.

The coming of humankind brought something that had not been seen before—the wonderful gift of self-consciousness. I think that the appearance of consciousness is the most remarkable thing that has happened in the whole of the fifteen-billion-year history of the universe that is known to us. That universe has become aware of itself. Death had been there for a very long time, but now there were beings who knew that they were going to die. At the same time that self-consciousness dawned, I believe that God-consciousness dawned also. The creation had become aware of its Creator. For some reason, lost to us now in the mists of pre-history, these new beings turned away from God and into themselves. They accepted that alienation from him which we thought about yesterday. That is what Christian doctrine calls the Fall.

Death had been in the world for millions of years but now it was perceived as mortality. Human beings became aware that they were going to die and, because they had lost contact with the One whose steadfast love was the ground of the hope for a destiny beyond death, that realization was a bitter one for them. Thorns and thistles, and all the other things which frustrate our intentions, were now experienced as making life empty and futile.

The nature of the earth did not change when men and women appeared on it, but they saw life in a way that made it seem hostile and meaningless. The truth of the matter is that without God the universe does not make sense. All its wonderful fruitfulness, and the beautiful order that science discovers, will ultimately seem pointless, because all is subject to change and decay. A godless world is one in which we cannot feel at home.

But we do not need to look at life in this way. There *is* a God; the universe *does* make sense; death does not have the last word. Yesterday, in many churches, priests will have taken ashes and made the sign of the cross on the foreheads of the worshippers, saying, 'You are dust, and to dust you shall return.' Looked at from the outside, that seems like a ceremony of despair, but experienced from the inside it is, in fact, the basis of our hope. Death is certainly real and we are not to pretend otherwise. Yet the only ultimate reality is God himself and he will not be defeated by human mortality. Lent is a time for trying to face a little more reality. We are creatures of dust but God has given us an intimation of immortality, a promise, that he is God 'not of the dead, but of the living' (Mark 12:27).

PRAYER

Lord, as we look on life and see that all things change and that all must die, help us to see beyond the flux of this decaying world to your unchangeable and certain purposes of steadfast love.

CHRISTIAN HUMANISM

Philippians 4 : 8 – 9

*Finally, beloved, whatever is true, whatever is
honourable, whatever is just, whatever is pure, whatever
is pleasing, whatever is commendable, if there is any
excellence and if there is anything worthy of praise, think
about these things. Keep on doing the things that you
have learned and received and heard and seen in me,
and the God of peace will be with you.*

These words of St Paul are a charter of Christian human-
ism, endorsing the value of all that is good and true in
human creativity and human action. We are not called to
live in some narrowly defined religious ghetto. We are to
rejoice and participate in all the richness of life. Those who
think of Paul as a kind of fanatical killjoy are shown here
how mistaken they have been.

The call to accept the true and honourable and just is
one that we need to pay particular attention to today. That
is because we are continually deluged with the false, the
dishonourable, the unjust. Even more insidious than the
pornography of violence and explicit sex is the tacit
assumption underlying so much presentation of life on
television and in novels, that there are no higher purposes
than the immediate gratification of our instinctive desires.
Of course, people commit a bit of adultery on the side
when they think they can get away with it... Of course, the
expression of our raw personality is more important than

the feelings or needs of those with whom we come into contact... Of course, if we can wangle something we're not entitled to, then why shouldn't we seize the opportunity? All the time, these morally corrupt role models are presented to us, without question, as the natural way to behave.

I am not arguing for a saccharine sweet, winsomely benevolent, destructively self-punishing kind of role model in their place. The trouble with both these depictions is their unreality. They trade in fantasy. We are back where we have been all this week, with the question of facing up to the way things are.

Someone once said that the attraction of soap operas is that they present a world in which deeds have no abiding moral consequences. Characters can betray each other, or hurt each other, in today's episode but be back exactly where they were in the next episode tomorrow. The real world is not like that. Great literature has always portrayed reality as it actually is, in its ability to bruise and to comfort. People do get caught in loveless marriages and seek the escape that adultery seems to offer, but infidelity cannot be free of the destructiveness that accompanies any act of betrayal. That is what Tolstoy's great novel *Anna Karenina* is about. Faithfulness and restraint are not costless virtues. They can be very painful in their consequences for those who hold to them. But no one will live truly and honourably without them.

There are black threads in the tapestry of life, but there are many golden ones also. We should be clear-eyed enough to see the glory as well as the sadness of the world, to rejoice in nature and friendship and art and simple goodness. There are many things worthy of praise for us to think upon.

PRAYER

Lord, we thank you for the riches of your creation. Help us to be true, honourable, just and pure, rejoicing in your gifts to us and faithful in our lives.

TRUTH AND TESTING

1 Thessalonians 5:21

... but test everything; hold fast to what is good...

The first epistle to the Thessalonians is probably the earliest document in the New Testament, having been written about AD50. St Paul has been talking about how to deal with prophets. Not all of them are quite what they seem to be and so the Thessalonians are encouraged to 'test everything'. I don't think we shall be misusing Paul if we take his advice more widely and treat it as an encouragement to careful inquiry in our search for religious truth of all kinds.

Let me say again something that I said in the Introduction but which is important enough to bear repetition. People sometimes seem to think that faith is a question of shutting your eyes, gritting your teeth and believing all sorts of strange and impossible things simply because some authority tells you to do so. That is a very bad mistake. The question of truth is of absolute importance in religion. The leap of faith is intended to be a leap into the light of knowledge and not into the darkness of superstition. We are to seek reasons for our beliefs and only to believe what is actually true.

The idea of testing everything is one that is very congenial to a scientist. In fact, I think that science and religion share a common concern in wanting to find out the truth about reality. However, it is very different aspects of reality which are the subjects of their respective inquiries. Science is looking at reality as an object, treating the world as an 'it'. That is why it can use experiments to bang things together and see what happens, or pull them apart and look at the pieces. Religion is concerned with personal encounter; it treats reality as a 'thou'. If I am always setting little traps to see if you are my friend, I shall soon destroy the possibility of friendship between us. That is because trust has to be the basis of any personal encounter. It's no use setting traps for God—praying that you'll get £1,000 in the post tomorrow and not believing in him if it doesn't happen. He won't play that sort of silly game. Testing divine truth can only come about by trusting divine graciousness. And then, as we learn something of God's goodness, we shall have to hold fast to what we have learned, committing ourselves to a life of faithful obedience to the truth which has been shown us.

One of the things that authors really like doing is signing copies of their books for the people that have bought them. Sometimes someone asks you to do a little more than just write your name and sometimes you feel you'd like to do that anyway, even without being asked. Very often, in these circumstances, I simply write '1 Thess. 5:21'. I hope that the person will be sufficiently curious to look the text up. It is one of my favourites because it emphasizes that searching for truth, which underlay my life as a scientist and continues to underlie my life as a Christian believer. Those of us who serve the God of truth should never fear the truth, from whatever source it comes but, having tested it, we should hold it fast with gratitude.

P R A Y E R

Lord Jesus, you are yourself the Truth we seek. Help us to test our understanding and to hold fast to that which we have found to be good.

EVIDENCE

1 Corinthians 15:1–8

Now I would remind you, brothers and sisters, of the good news that I proclaimed to you, which you in turn received, in which also you stand, through which also you are being saved, if you hold firmly to the message that I proclaimed to you—unless you have come to believe in vain. For I handed on to you as of first importance what I in turn had received: that Christ died for our sins in accordance with the scriptures, and that he was buried, and that he was raised on the third day in accordance with the scriptures, and that he appeared to Cephas, then to the twelve. Then he appeared to more than five hundred brothers and sisters at one time, most of whom are still alive, though some have died. Then he appeared to James, then to all the apostles. Last of all, as to one untimely born, he appeared also to me.

Today's passage is the earliest account we have of the resurrection. St Paul wrote his first letter to the Corinthians in the middle fifties AD, about twenty to twenty-five years after the crucifixion and at least ten years before St Mark's Gospel. He reminds them of what he had told them when he founded the church in Corinth a few years earlier. When he says he handed on to them what he had himself received, Paul is no doubt referring to his instruction in the faith following his conversion on the Damascus road. That takes us back to within two or three years of the crucifixion. This is very early evidence indeed.

Mostly it is in the form of a long list of witnesses who had seen the risen Jesus, ending with Paul himself. (The fact that Peter is referred to by his Aramaic name Cephas, rather than the Greek *Petros* which soon became common, is a little confirming sign of how ancient this material is.) Most of these people were still alive when Paul was writing his letter. There is a clear appeal to human testimony to the truth of the resurrection.

You might wonder why no women are mentioned in the list, since the later accounts in the Gospels give them a prominent role. I think that the answer is precisely because Paul was here concerned with establishing the evidence for the resurrection appearances. In the ancient world, women had a depressed status and their testimony was not acceptable as evidence in a court of law. So on this occasion they were just left out.

People sometimes say that Paul talks about appearances of the risen Christ but he never refers to the empty tomb, so maybe these latter stories (which are in all four Gospels) were made up later on. I'd want to say two things in reply to that. One is that the only writings of Paul that we have are some of his letters. Paul never sat down to write out all he knew but he simply mentioned things as they seemed appropriate to the theme of the letter in hand. It's very dangerous to conclude that he didn't know more than has survived in these bits of correspondence. The other thing is to draw attention to a curious item in this brief passage.

Paul is repeating a very concise formula. It's a kind of early creed, stating basic belief in the fundamental Christian event of the resurrection. No words are wasted. Yet, in this very condensed account, space is found to tell us that Jesus was buried. Why bother with that unless it was known that there was something special about the tomb? That specialness was not that the burial site of Jesus was an honoured place of pilgrimage (as was the case for many Jewish heroes), but surely it was that for him the burial site was an irrelevancy. There had been a tomb but it was now empty! In this oblique way, I think we can see a hint that Paul knew about the tomb's emptiness. In fact, I believe it would have been impossible for a first-century Jew to believe that Jesus was alive but yet his body mouldered on in the grave.

There is evidence for the resurrection. That evidence carries us back to the very earliest days of the Christian movement. As a matter of fact, I think that there would have been no such movement at all if the resurrection had not taken place. Jesus' life ended in apparent defeat and failure. His followers deserted him and ran away. Something tremendous must have happened to turn those frightened men into the proclaimers that Jesus was God's Lord and Christ. If he had not been raised from the dead, I believe we would never have heard of Jesus.

P R A Y E R

Lord Jesus, as your first disciples bore a joyful witness to your resurrection, so may we, who have not seen you but yet believe, manifest your power in our lives and testify to your conquering of death.

CREATION

IN THE BEGINNING

Genesis 1 : 1 – 5

*In the beginning when God created the heavens and the
earth, the earth was a formless void and darkness covered
the face of the deep, while a wind from God swept over
the face of the waters. Then God said, 'Let there be light';
and there was light. And God saw that the light was
good; and God separated the light from the darkness.
God called the light Day, and the darkness he called
Night. And there was evening and there was morning,
the first day.*

In this famous passage of scripture we read words which
many people seem to think result in a head-on collision
between science and religion, with science emerging
unscathed and religion being killed stone dead. After all,
don't we know that really in the beginning it was the Big
Bang?

If you think that Genesis was written solely as a blow-by-
blow account of the history of the universe, then of course
you're bound to conclude that it has a lot of mistakes in it
(how could you have plants before there was the sun to
give its light to make them grow—see days three and four)
and modern science has done an infinitely better job. But,
wait a minute! It can't be as simple as that. After all, there
are *two* very different creation stories in Genesis, one in the
first chapter and a more ancient and primitive one in the
second chapter. If the final editor of the book thought it

was just about cosmic history, why were two incompatible versions included, side by side? That's a clue to encourage us to think that we should look for a different understanding of what Genesis is about. It's not an early and inadequate scientific textbook at all. It's something altogether different, and in fact more interesting.

The central assertion of the first chapter of Genesis is that God said, 'Let there be...'. It occurs eight times, in one form or another, in the course of the chapter. The purpose of the book is not to tell us what happened but *why* it happened. The world exists because of the will of God, its Creator. His mind and purpose lie behind its fruitful history. Genesis 1 may contain elements of ancient science, now superseded, but its primary purpose is theological, and that message has not become out of date.

As a matter of fact, the more we've learned about cosmology, the more it seems to me to reveal a universe filled with the rumour of a divine will behind it. The wonderful order and pattern of the physical world that science has discovered corresponds to a universe shot through with signs of mind. Its fruitful history has only been possible because the forces of nature take very specific forms, permitting such diverse phenomena as stars which shine steadily for billions of years (and so provide energy for the evolution of life) or ice which floats on water (rather than sinking to the bottom and so killing all aquatic life as lakes froze solid). Of course, there are many things which could have happened differently. Human beings did not have to have five fingers. But that conscious life of some kind has developed does not appear to be at all chancy. That possibility seems to have been built into the very fabric of physical law from the beginning.

Science tells us how all this has happened, but it is unable to tell us why it has happened. I am not at all inclined to treat cosmic fruitfulness and order as strokes of accidental good luck. If I am to understand the world I need the insights of religion into its status as a creation quite as much as I need the insights of science into its physical process.

The fire is burning in the hearth because chemical processes are releasing energy as heat. The fire is burning in the hearth as a sign of welcome—come and join me round it. I do not have to choose between these two descriptions. Both are true and I need both if I am to understand what is going on.

In the beginning, was the Big Bang. In the beginning, God said, 'Let there be...'. I do not need to choose between these two statements. I need both if I am truly to understand the wonderful world in which we live.

PRAYER

We praise you, O God, for the order and fertility of your creation, for the discoveries of science about its history and pattern, and for the insights of those who have seen your hand at work as its Creator.

EVOLUTION

Genesis 2:4–9

These are the generations of the heavens and the earth when they were created. In the day that the Lord God made the earth and the heavens, when no plant of the field was yet in the earth and no herb of the field had yet sprung up—for the Lord God had not caused it to rain upon the earth, and there was no one to till the ground; but a stream would rise from the earth, and water the whole face of the ground—then the Lord God formed man from the dust of the ground, and breathed into his nostrils the breath of life; and the man became a living being. And the Lord God planted a garden in Eden, in the east; and there he put the man whom he had formed. Out of the ground the Lord God made to grow every tree that is pleasant to the sight and good for food, the tree of life also in the midst of the garden, and the tree of the knowledge of good and evil.

It may seem pretty odd to preface talking about evolution by quoting from the second chapter of Genesis. The latter gives an ancient, and we may think naive, account of humanity being made by God, the master craftsman. Yet it is from the dust of the ground (Hebrew: *adamah*) that Adam is made. More than a pun is involved here. Humanity's continuity with nature is being asserted in a plain and striking way. That is half the story. The other half is that God 'breathed into his nostrils the breath of life; and the man became a living being'. The Hebrew word for living being can also be used of animals, but humankind's special status is made clear later on in the story when the animals are brought to Adam so that he can give them their names. Animals and people belong together, but there is a special status for humans which is symbolized by this story of the naming ceremony.

The scientific account of evolution also pictures man and women as descended from the dust of the ground, through the long history of life on earth connecting *homo sapiens* to the chemically rich shallow pools in which the first replicating molecules are thought to have originated, three to four billion years ago. It is sad that so much unnecessary conflict between science and religion has centred on Darwin's theory, and sadder still that this confrontation continues today in the creationist controversies of North America.

Remember that yesterday we were thinking that science is concerned with asking 'How?' and religion is concerned with asking 'Why?' questions. Evolutionary theory tells us how God's creative purposes have been fulfilled in the history of life on earth. Theology has no real difficulty in living with science's answer. No doubt God could have created everything ready-made, if that is what he had wanted to do. In fact, however, he has chosen to do something cleverer than that. An evolutionary world is to be understood theologically as a world allowed by its Creator *to make itself*. The fruitfulness of creation has been brought to maturity through the shuffling explorations of possibility which we call evolutionary history. Creation is not something that God did, once and for all, a long time in the past. It is something that he has been doing all the time and that he is continuing to do today. When you stop to think about it, that's the way one might have expected the God of love to be at work. He will not just snap his fingers in a magical sort of way and force things to happen, just like that. The God of love is patient and subtle and he will allow his creation to make itself.

The fact that we have emerged from the dust of the ground does not mean that we are merely material creatures. In our nostrils is also the breath of the divine life. We have kinship with the animals, but we are more than merely animal in our nature. I am an unrepentant speciesist—that is, I believe that humans are different from and superior to the rest of the animal creation. Men and women are self-conscious, moral, worshipping, sinful beings, all qualities which the animals do not possess. We are something new in the creative purposes of God.

P R A Y E R

*Lord, we are made from the dust of the ground.
Help us to care for the natural world that has given
us birth. Lord, we have your breath of life in our
nostrils. May it inspire us to love and serve you.*

HUMANITY IN NATURE

Psalm 104:19–23

You have made the moon to mark the seasons;
the sun knows its time for setting.
You make darkness, and it is night, when all the animals
of the forest come creeping out.
The young lions roar for their prey, seeking their food
from God.
When the sun rises, they withdraw and lie down in
their dens.
People go out to their work and to their labour until the
evening.

We need to remember that there is a good deal about creation in the Bible and most of it is outside the first chapters of Genesis. Some of it is in the Psalms, most notably in Psalm 104. It is well worth reading the whole of this psalm, which gives a long description of the beauties and wonders of the natural world. People play a very modest role in this account, only really appearing in verse 23, which emphasizes the role of human labour.

It's a useful corrective for us to be put in our place once in a while. A great deal of theological talk, in church and outside it, is solely concentrated on men and women. I'm not suggesting that humankind is unimportant. I'm sure that we are of very great significance in God's eyes and that he cares for each one of us. Yet we are not the whole of creation. Nature is not there just to be pretty scenery in front of which the human play is being performed. The Bible encourages us to look at nature and to remember that our Creator cares for it too.

First, the Bible looks at nature with a clear, unsentimental gaze. It knows that 'the young lions roar for their prey', going on to assert that they are 'seeking their food from God'. Nature is ambiguous. It is not all red in tooth and claw, but neither is it full of cuddly furry animals who are strictly vegetarian. It is an exciting but strange world in which we live.

Secondly, humans intervene in nature. When they go out to their labour, part of that work is no doubt the cultivation of the soil. Gardeners know three things. One is that you have to respect nature and cooperate with it. It is no good trying to grow acid-loving plants like azaleas in the limey soil of Cambridgeshire. Such efforts are condemned to futility. The second thing that gardeners know is that you cannot just leave it to nature. Weeds will soon choke the garden if you do so. There is a battle to be fought, invasive plants to be restrained, pests to be eliminated. We have natural foes in our encounters with nature as well as natural friends. The third thing is that gardeners come to love and honour the beauty of the living world. There is immense satisfaction to be had in watching the growth of plants and the changing colourings of the seasons.

I think we should take seriously the image given us in Genesis 3 of people living in a garden. It will help us to take a balanced view about how human beings should relate to the rest of creation. There is a duty of respect and there is a right to exercise control. The two are reconciled with each other in the kind of stewardly care which successful gardening requires. Without gardeners, there would be no gardens. But without plants and insects there would be no gardens either.

PRAYER

Lord help us to use your creation aright, to love and respect your other creatures and to cooperate with you in the continuing life of your world.

A MATHEMATICAL UNIVERSE

Psalm 111:2

Great are the works of the Lord, studied by all who delight in them.

When the Cavendish Laboratory was founded at Cambridge University in 1871, its first professor was James Clerk Maxwell. He was one of the greatest theoretical physicists of all time, whose researches had established the character of electromagnetic forces and given great insight into the nature of light. Maxwell was also a deeply Christian man. He had this verse from the Psalms, in its Latin version, carved over the archway leading to his laboratory. I am glad to say that when the Cavendish moved some years ago into large modern buildings on the outskirts of Cambridge, the Psalmist's words were again reproduced over its entrance.

Some people might be surprised at that, because they hold the mistaken view that science and religion are somehow at war with each other. As a matter of fact, scientists are quite often religious believers and that is noticeably so among theoretical physicists. There are many reasons why this is the case, but one of them is that we live in a mathematical universe which certainly looks like a world with a mind behind it.

Mathematics is not everyone's cup of tea and if it's not yours just think of it as being a way of investigating patterns. Time and again it has turned out that the most beautiful patterns of mathematics are just those which describe the structure of the universe. Somehow our minds and the world fit together in this wonderful way.

I suppose that the greatest theoretical physicist I've known personally was Paul Dirac. He's not very well known to the general public but he was one of the founding fathers of quantum theory and a very great man indeed. As it happens, he was not a religious person but he spent his life in the search for beautiful equations, because he knew that they would be the ones which had a chance of describing what the universe is like. If you're not a mathematician, you may find the notion of beautiful equations to be rather a strange idea. I'll have to ask you to believe me that mathematical beauty, like other kinds of beauty, is something which is hard to describe but easy to recognize, if you're lucky enough to have been given the eyes to see it. And you'll have to believe me also when I tell you that we've never discovered a fundamental physical theory which was expressed in ugly mathematics. The world is mathematically beautiful!

Most of the time we take the possibility of science for granted, but when you stop to think about it it's surely remarkable that we can understand the world so well and that mathematics is the key to unlock its secrets. Einstein once said that the only incomprehensible thing about the universe is that it is comprehensible. Why is science possible? You can't find certain, knock-down answers to deep questions like that, but here's my reply. Science is possible because the universe is a creation and we are creatures made in the image of our Creator. When scientists like Stephen Hawking talk about physics helping us to know something of the mind of God, they are speaking more truthfully than maybe they realize.

P R A Y E R

Lord, bless those who delight in your works and seek to understand the workings of your creation. May they honour you, the one whose mind is the ground of the wonderful order that they discover, and may they use their knowledge for the good of all your people.

GOD'S PURPOSES

Job 38:1-7

Then the Lord answered Job out of the whirlwind:
'Who is this that darkens counsel by words without
  knowledge?
Gird up your loins like a man, I will question you, and
you shall declare to me.
Where were you when I laid the foundation of the earth?
Tell me, if you have understanding.
Who determined its measurements—surely you know!
Or who stretched the line upon it?
On what were its bases sunk, or who laid its cornerstone
when the morning stars sang together
  and all the heavenly beings shouted for joy?'

Ancient Israel never developed anything that looked at all like science. In this they differed from the Babylonians (who were excellent astronomers) and the Greeks (who thought about everything). The nearest Israel got to science was in the wisdom writings, which take a cool look at what is going on in the world. The greatest of these writings is the book of Job. We all know the story. Great disasters impinge on Job and he loses his family, his riches, his health. His friends think it must be because he has offended God in some way. Job insists that he is innocent. The argument rolls on for thirty-seven chapters. Then, in chapter thirty-eight, the Lord himself answers Job from out of the whirlwind. What he has to say is very surprising.

God doesn't explain to Job what has been going on or offer him comfort in his distress. Instead, for four chapters, the Lord tells Job to look up and see all the wonderful things God is doing in the world. And in the end, Job is content. God himself is the sufficient answer.

There seem to be two main points about this reply. One is to enlarge Job's understanding of God to take in a little more of God's majesty and power. J.B. Phillips once wrote a book called *Your God is Too Small*. We all of us have miniature pictures of God, theological scale models which are quite inadequate to the grandeur of the divine nature. We need to look up. Take one rather trivial example from science: the vastness of the universe. Our sun is one ordinary star among the hundred thousand million stars of our galaxy, the Milky Way, which is just one among the hundred thousand million galaxies of the observable universe. The universe is unimaginably big. We shouldn't be upset at this vastness—the cosmologists tell us that only a universe as big as this one could last the fifteen billion years it takes to make men and women—but we should let the heavens declare to us the glory of their Creator. Who knows what other purposes he has at work in this vast world that he holds in being?

The second point is one that we have encountered before. God cares for human beings but he cares for the rest of nature also. We matter to him but we are not the only things that matter. Towards the end of the speech from the whirlwind, God refers to a mythical monster called Behemoth. This monster is a symbol standing for the otherness of non-human creation. God says to Job, 'Look at Behemoth, which I made just as I made you' (40:15). In other words, don't think, Job, that you're the only one I have concern for. I have purposes for all my creatures, which go far beyond what you can imagine.

PRAYER

O Lord our God, you are great and wonderful.
Enlarge our vision of your majesty and power and
assure us of your purposes for us and for all your
creatures.

CHANCE

Job 41:1–2, 31–34

'Can you draw out Leviathan with a fishhook,
*   or press down its tongue with a cord?*
Can you put a rope in its nose,
*   or pierce its jaw with a hook?...*
It makes the deep boil like a pot;
*   it makes the sea like a pot of ointment.*
It leaves a shining wake behind it;
*   one would think the deep to be white-haired.*
On earth it has no equal,
*   a creature without fear.*
It surveys everything that is lofty;
*   it is king over all that are proud.'*

There is a second mythical monster referred to in the book of Job. He is Leviathan, a chaos monster. The Hebrews feared the waters of chaos which they saw as continually threatening the order of the land. They did not like the sea.

For us, Leviathan can stand for the role of chance in the process of the world. Many people today dislike the idea of chance and think that its presence is a sign that everything is meaningless. I think they are mistaken.

'Chance' is a slippery word and we have to make sure we know what lies behind it. When people talk about chance operating in the physical world, there are a number of senses in which it is being used. One is the simple historical fact that this happened rather than that. This particular genetic mutation occurred and life moved in this particular direction. Other mutations would have been possible, and if it had been one of them which had happened, life would have taken a somewhat different course. There is no doubt that this sort of chance—which should really be called contingency—has operated all the time. We might have had six fingers rather than five. What this tells us is that the history of the universe has been more like an acted-out improvisation than the performance of a totally predetermined script. We have already thought that an evolutionary world is one that is allowed to make itself. The universe is not God's puppet theatre in which he pulls every string. The God of love could not be such a cosmic tyrant. Used in this sense, chance is something positive, for it represents the room for manoeuvre that the Creator has given to his creatures in allowing them to be themselves.

A second sense of chance relates to the unpredictabilities of what is going on. We call the fall of dice 'chance' because we can't calculate what the result will be. Modern physics has shown that there is a lot of this sort of chance around. It is there, not only in the uncertainties which quantum theory ascribes to atomic processes, but also in the cloudy unpredictabilities of most everyday events, which the quite recent discoveries of what is called chaos theory have brought to light. The weather is so sensitive to small disturbances that a butterfly stirring the air in the African jungle today could have consequences for storms over England in three or four weeks time!

The old clockwork, mechanical picture of the physical world is well and truly dead. In its place there is something that is more supple and more subtle. I think that we should understand these widespread unpredictabilities, not as meaning that the world is somehow meaninglessly random, but that it is open to other kinds of causes in addition to those described by physics alone. I think that is how we act in the world. I think that it is how God acts in world history also.

Leviathan may look like a frightening monster. Chance might seem to threaten meaning. But actually this is not so. Chance is a way of referring to the openness of reality, the character of that world in which God is ceaselessly at work and in which we are given the opportunity of cooperating with him.

P R A Y E R

Help us, Lord, among the changes and chances and opportunities of this world, always to rely upon your unchanging steadfast love.

NEW CREATION

Revelation 21:3–5a; 2 Corinthians 5:17

*And I heard a loud voice from the throne saying, 'See,
the home of God is among mortals. He will dwell with
them as their God; they will be his peoples, and God
himself will be with them; he will wipe every tear from
their eyes. Death will be no more; mourning and crying
and pain will be no more, for the first things have passed
away.' And the one who was seated on the throne said,
'See, I am making all things new.'*

*So if anyone is in Christ, there is a new creation:
everything old has passed away; see, everything has
become new!*

We are all going to die. A hundred years hence no one
reading this page will still be alive. The universe itself is
going to die. Either it will collapse into a fiery melting pot
or it will decay into low-grade radiation. That death will
take a little longer. It won't happen for many billions of
years, but it will certainly happen in the end. Ultimately all
is condemned to futility.

It looks a pretty bleak prospect. In the search for truth
we have to face the fact of mortality. But the last word does
not lie with death. The last word belongs to God alone. As
Christians we believe that he has already spoken that word.
The old creation will die but God will bring about a
new creation in which death and sorrow will have been

abolished for ever. For the fact is, in Christ that new creation has already begun. The resurrection of Jesus is the seed from which the redeemed order will grow.

These are wonderful thoughts of hope. What reason do we have to believe them? Do they make sense?

We have two reasons for believing that they are true. The first reason is the faithfulness of God. He will not abandon that which he loves. He will never allow death to defeat his benevolent purposes. The second reason is, of course, the resurrection of Jesus. God has shown us by a great act within history what he intends for all of us beyond history.

Does such a hope make sense? When we die, isn't that just the end of us? In order to answer that question you have to decide what is the real me. In other words, what is the soul? Many people used to think that it was a spiritual component that got detached at death and was carried up to heaven. I find it hard to think that way today. The effect of brain injuries or drugs on how we think and behave seems to emphasize that our bodies are an essential part of us. That wouldn't have surprised the writers of the Bible, for the Hebrews thought in exactly the same way. They believed that a person without a body was just a sort of ghostly shade. That doesn't mean, however, that we are simply material beings either. The atoms in our bodies are changing all the time through eating and drinking, wear and tear. Of themselves, they are of no significance. What is the real me, what maintains continuity during all those changes of atoms, is the dynamic *pattern* in which those atoms are organized. That is what the soul is: the unimaginably complex pattern of animated matter which is you or which is me. I believe it makes perfect sense to believe that after my death God remembers the pattern that is me and that he will recreate it in his final great act of resurrection. In a very crude and inadequate analogy, you could say that the real me is the software, currently running on the perishable hardware of this world, but capable of being transferred to the imperishable hardware of the world to come.

PRAYER

Finish then thy new creation;
pure and spotless let us be;
let us see thy great salvation,
perfectly restored in thee;
changed from glory into glory,
till in heaven we take our place,
till we cast our crowns before thee,
lost in wonder, love and praise.

Charles Wesley

REALITY

A MORAL WORLD

Psalm 19:1–2, 7–9

The heavens are telling the glory of God;
and the firmament proclaims his handiwork.
Day to day pours forth speech,
and night to night declares knowledge...
The law of the Lord is perfect, reviving the soul;
the decrees of the Lord are sure, making wise the simple;
the precepts of the Lord are right, rejoicing the heart;
the commandment of the Lord is clear, enlightening the
    eyes;
the fear of the Lord is pure, enduring for ever;
the ordinances of the Lord are true and righteous
    altogether.

Psalm 19 falls into two parts. The first six verses are about
the physical world and its wonders. The remaining eight
verses remind us that this same universe is also a moral
world. That fact is surely one of great significance and
importance.

Knowledge of reality comes to us in many ways. Science
tells us a lot about how things happen, but the world that
it describes is cold, lifeless, impersonal. By itself that could
never be an adequate account of reality. We have other
sources of knowledge and one of them is our moral sense
of right and wrong. I believe that I know as surely as I
know anything that love is better than hate, truth is better
than lying, that torturing children is wrong. I cannot for

one moment think that these insights are just conventions of our particular society, so that we have simply decided as a matter of taste not to subject children to the rack and to the thumbscrew. A moral issue like not telling lies is something quite different from a cultural issue like not wishing to eat horse meat. There are all sorts of these cultural conditionings at work in the choices we make but underlying them is a true moral knowledge of right and wrong which is part of our encounter with the reality of the world.

Of course, some people think that these feelings of moral imperative are just rules for survival built into us over the history of evolution by our selfish genes. We care for our children simply to ensure the continuance of our genetic inheritance. This seems to me to be a most implausible idea. When someone endangers their life by rushing into a burning building in order to attempt to rescue some unknown person to whom they are in no way related, we rightly honour their courage and admire their selflessness. It is impossible to understand this ethical act in terms of some implicit calculation of genetic advantage.

How then does it come about that this physical world, made up of matter and energy, is also the arena for moral choices made according to our deepest intuitions of right and wrong? There must be much more to reality than science has been able to describe in its own self-limited terms of physical cause and effect. There must be a spiritual dimension corresponding to our experiences as moral beings. I believe that our intuitions of ethical demands are intimations of the good and perfect will of our Creator. We are moral beings because we are creatures in a world created by a God of love and justice.

This way of thinking about morality illustrates how a belief in God provides a deeper understanding of reality than we would be able to attain without a religious faith. Our atheist friends are not stupid, and many of them are seeking to live upright and good lives, but they are able to explain less than theists can.

P R A Y E R

Let the words of my mouth and the meditation of my heart be acceptable to you, O Lord, my rock and my redeemer.

Psalm 19:14

BEAUTY

Psalm 150:3-6

Praise him with trumpet sound;
  praise him with lute and harp!
Praise him with tambourine and dance;
  praise him with strings and pipe!
Praise him with clanging cymbals;
  praise him with loud clashing cymbals!
Let everything that breathes praise the Lord!
Praise the Lord!

Ask a scientist, as a scientist, to tell you what music is and he or she will reply that it is vibrations in the air. From the scientific point of view, that is all that can be said. Yet we all know that there is much more to music than that, just as a great painting is more than a collection of spots of paint of known chemical composition. In the case of a beautiful object, science can give a description which in its own terms leaves nothing out, but which from the point of view of reality leaves almost everything out. Once again we see that there is a many-layered richness present in this world in which we live.

I am sure that we should take our experiences of beauty extremely seriously. They are a window onto reality through which we need to look. I am particularly fascinated by the mystery of music: that a succession of sounds in time can conspire harmoniously together to produce in our hearts an intimation of eternity. At various periods of my life when I have been feeling harassed or depressed, I have experienced the wordless power of music to convey peace and hope. J.S. Bach speaks to me in this way beyond all other composers. I write as someone who is musically ill-educated and completely ungifted. Nevertheless, even for me, music can touch a depth within me.

There is really little else to say. The point is precisely the existence of this non-verbal access to value which the arts provide for us. The best thing to do now would be to listen to a favourite piece of music, or look at a much-loved picture, or simply gaze out of the window at the beauty of nature if you are lucky enough to have that close to you.

Why is the world beautiful? Where does this extra dimension to reality come from? Once more we are being pointed beyond the merely material to the spiritual. There is beauty in the world because it is a creation. Our experiences of delight are sharings in the Creator's joy in his creation.

P R A Y E R

*Open our eyes, Lord, to perceive true beauty, pure
and unalloyed, and seeing it, to rejoice and give
thanks to you, who are its Creator.*

WONDER

Proverbs 30:18-19

Three things are too wonderful for me;
four I do not understand:
the way of an eagle in the sky,
the way of a snake on a rock,
the way of a ship on the high seas,
and the way of a man with a girl.

The writers who contributed to the book of Proverbs were on the whole pretty steady, unemotional sort of people. They tried to look at things coolly and with detachment and to see them as they are. They are very matter of fact, saying things such as, 'Like a gold ring in a pig's snout is a beautiful woman without good sense' (11:22) and, 'A soft answer turns away wrath, but a harsh word stirs up anger' (15:1). Yet even they can be shaken out of their common-sense equilibrium by the sense of wonder that the world evokes.

Our list of wonderful things would probably be rather different from theirs, but we would be living very impoverished lives if we were dead to all sense of wonder at what is going on around us. You might think that scientists are also on the whole pretty steady, unemotional sort of people. In many ways they are, but they too are certainly no strangers to the sense of wonder.

Scientific research, like any other kind of worthwhile activity, is full of boring routine and frustrating blind alleys. Theoretical physicists generate a lot of crumpled pieces of paper as what seemed like good ideas fail to work out quite right. The pay-off for all this weary activity is the sense of wonder as, once in a while, some new aspect of the physical world becomes understood by us. I was reading recently a history of a certain episode of discovery in my old subject, elementary particle physics. I could relive again the excitement and satisfaction in our community as a particularly neat pattern of physical behaviour had become clear to us. Einstein once wrote about the experience of marvelling at the delicate web of relationships revealed in nature, that it meant that 'in every true searcher of Nature there is a kind of religious reverence'.

When scientists enjoy the sense of wonder in this way, whether they know it or not, they are praising God for the magnificence of his creation. To experience wonder is to utter an implicit prayer of thankfulness to the One whose majesty we have just succeeded in glimpsing. Creation is inexhaustibly rich. At every level, the personal, the domestic, the natural, the cosmic, there are things to be discovered that will fill our hearts with joy and gladness. They will show us that we and all creation are fearfully and wonderfully made.

PRAYER

Great and amazing are your deeds,
Lord God the Almighty!
Just and true are your ways,
King of the nations!
Lord, who will not fear
and glorify your name?
For you alone are holy.

Revelation 15:3–4

PRAISE

Psalm 145:1–3

I will extol you, my God and King,
and bless your name for ever and ever.
Every day I will bless you,
and praise your name for ever and ever.
Great is the Lord, and greatly to be praised;
his greatness is unsearchable.

It is natural to move from wonder to praise. The acknowledgment of God's greatness, which is implicit in the one,
is made explicit in the other. It is not surprising that music
plays so large a part in the expression of our thankfulness
through songs of praise.

There is a danger here, however. We all like a good sing,
even if all we can manage personally is the somewhat
untuneful bawlings of the faithful. The latter are certainly
no less acceptable to God than the perhaps somewhat
routine perfection of a professional choir. Yet we must be
careful not simply to be carried away with the emotion of
the moment, so to enjoy the praising that we actually forget
the One whose praise we are singing. There has to be a
reflective sobriety in praise as well as an expressive rejoicing.

The greatest treasury of praise available to us is the book
of Psalms. Each of these poems is more than 2,000 years
old and over the centuries they have been the staple diet of
worship, both for the Jewish community in which they
originated and for the Christian church. Their riches seem

inexhaustible. Many religious (that is, monks and nuns) say the whole Psalter in the course of a week's worship. As an Anglican priest, I work my way through the Psalms about every ten weeks through the recitation of the Daily Office. I gladly testify to the spiritual power that they bring.

It is very instructive to compare the Psalter to the hymn-book. The comparison is very much to the advantage of the Psalms. They are full of praise, but that does not blind the psalmists to the ambiguous character of the world in which we live. There are also many laments, arising from the experience of desolation and of suffering. The writers are very bold and honest in the expression of their feelings. They can even say 'Wake up!' to God: 'Rouse yourself! Why do you sleep, O Lord? Awake, do not cast us off forever!' (Psalm 44:23). There is a much wider and deeper range of spiritual experience expressed in the Psalms than I have ever found in any hymnbook. Using the Psalms for our praise is a perfect antidote to any superficial jollity in our honouring God. It would be a great tragedy if the current pattern of public worship used in many of our churches had the unintentional effect of making this spiritual storehouse unknown or inaccessible to many people

P R A Y E R

Praise the Lord!
Praise God in his sanctuary;
praise him in his mighty firmament!
Praise him for his mighty deeds;
praise him according to his surpassing greatness!

Psalm 150:1–2

NATURAL THEOLOGY

Romans 1:19-20

For what can be known about God is plain to them,
because God has shown it to them. Ever since the
creation of the world his eternal power and divine
nature, invisible though they are, have been understood
and seen through the things he has made.

This week we have been thinking about reality. We have seen that we must think of it in a broad and generous way if we are to do justice to its riches. Science only tells us about one aspect of the way things are. Our experiences of morality and beauty slip through the wide meshes of its net, but that does not at all mean that we should neglect the insights into our world that they provide. Those different levels of reality evoke in us a feeling of wonder at the plenitude of it all. If we are religious people, this will lead us to praise the Creator for the abundance and profundity of his creation.

Thinking along these lines is what is called natural theology—that is to say, trying to understand something of God from the character of his creation, using our minds and our experience to sample its riches. These verses from the opening chapter of St Paul's epistle to the Romans show that this is an activity with a long history.

We do not expect to find the universe full of things stamped 'Made by God'. The Creator is more subtle than that. Yet is would be surprising if there were no hints accessible to us that a mind and purpose lies behind it all. When one is attempting to discuss deep questions, such as whether God exists, there is no simple, knock-down way of arguing. I do not think it is possible to prove that God exists, any more than it is possible to prove that he doesn't exist. The debate between theists and atheists is not like discussing whether 598 is the square root of 357,604. In questions of arithmetic there is a definite answer (it is), on which we should all be able to agree if we think clearly enough. Religious, or anti-religious, questions are much more subtle. They cannot be settled by logical demonstration, for the essence of what is at issue is whether it makes better overall sense of experience to believe that there is a divine mind and will behind it all or not to believe that. We can give motivations for our answer, one way or the other, but we cannot simply settle it by argument alone. In the end we have to commit ourselves to a chosen point of view.

I have already made it clear that I think that belief in God provides a much better explanation of reality than just supposing the world is there as a brute fact and there is nothing more to say about it. The fact that we live in a mathematical universe is made intelligible by recognizing the rationality of the Creator. The fact that we live in a moral world is made intelligible by recognizing the benevolent will of its Creator. The fact that we live in a world which is the carrier of beauty is made intelligible by recognizing the Creator's joy in the goodness of his creation. Theism makes sense of a lot of things which would otherwise seem to be strange but happy accidents.

One final word of warning. Natural theology is useful, but at best it is only a limited exercise. By itself it is not enough. If we are to know the God and Father of our Lord Jesus Christ, we shall have to leave the sphere of general discussion and take the risk of entering the sphere of personal encounter.

PRAYER

*Lord, help us to see your eternal power and
divine nature in the things that you have made,
and then lead us on to know you more fully as you
have made yourself known in your Son, our
Saviour Jesus Christ.*

THE WORLD TO COME

Revelation 21:1

Then I saw a new heaven and a new earth; for the first heaven and the first earth had passed away, and the sea was no more.

Reality is wider than the world of our personal direct experience. There is the reality of God, which we glimpse through scripture and prayer and discipleship. There is also the reality of the world to come, in which we place our hope—the new creation that we thought about last Sunday.

John tells us that in that new heaven and new earth there will not be any sea. A maritime people like the British might think that was a pity. We must, of course, understand the symbolism of what is being said. Revelation is the book in the New Testament most imbued with purely Jewish thought (it is full of echoes from the Old Testament) and to the Hebrew mind the sea represented the threatening waters of chaos. The absence of sea is a way of expressing what the writer spells out more clearly a little later on, that 'Death will be no more; mourning and crying and pain will be no more' (v. 4).

The world to come will be free from all the pain and sorrow which make this present world a vale of tears. If that were not the case, the life of the world to come would present a grim prospect rather than the fulfilment of Christian hope. There is one problem, however: if the new creation is going to be so wonderful, why did God bother with the old? If God can make a world free from pain and suffering, why didn't he do so the first time round?

This is a serious question which requires a serious answer. I believe that we should think about it this way. The present world, the old creation, is allowed by its Creator to be itself. The God of love gave it the gift of independence. We have already thought several times that our evolutionary universe is one that is allowed to make itself. We shall see later on that a world like that cannot be free from ragged edges and blind alleys. The world to come, the new creation, is something different. It will be a world in which God is welcomed and the divine presence will everywhere be manifested in a new and unveiled way. The present world contains sacraments, special focused events in which the presence of God is particularly experienced. The world to come will be wholly sacramental. It will be one in which God is 'all in all' (1 Corinthians 15:28). Such a world can be free from the corruption and mortality that are our present lot.

The new creation is the transformation and glorification of the old creation, just as the Lord's risen body was the transformation and glorification of his dead body. Jesus could not get to Easter without going through Good Friday. We cannot get to the new creation without passing through the vale of tears that is the old creation. We have to live this life before we reach the life of the world to come.

P R A Y E R

Lord, you have set before us a wonderful hope.
Be with us in the trials and tribulations of this
world, so that in the world to come our hurts may be
healed and we may see you face to face.

THE COSMIC CHRIST

Colossians 1:15–20

[Christ] is the image of the invisible God, the firstborn of all creation; for in him all things in heaven and on earth were created, things visible and invisible, whether thrones or dominions or rulers or powers—all things have been created through him and for him. He himself is before all things, and in him all things hold together. He is the head of the body, the church; he is the beginning, the firstborn from the dead, so that he might come to have first place in everything. For in him all the fullness of God was pleased to dwell, and through him God was pleased to reconcile to himself all things, whether on earth or in heaven, by making peace through the blood of his cross.

These verses make an astonishing and exciting claim: that Jesus Christ is of significance, not only for human life here on planet earth, but for the whole universe. He is of cosmic significance. In him 'all things in heaven and on earth were created', in him 'all things hold together', through him 'God was pleased to reconcile to himself all things'. Notice the reiteration of the words *all things*. Christ is not just the redeemer of human beings, he is the redeemer of everything that is.

At first sight it seems an unbelievably exaggerated claim to make. Could a wandering preacher in a peripheral province of the Roman empire be a person of significance for the Andromeda nebula and beyond? But as you start to think about it, and to consider the Christian belief that it was God who was at work in Christ reconciling the world to himself (2 Corinthians 5:19), then nothing less than this will really do. We have already had some hints pointing us in this direction.

The universe is going to die, but if God really cares for his creation, all of it must have an appropriate destiny beyond its death, just as we shall have. If Jesus is 'the first-born from the dead', then he is the prime source of all new life. Our destiny is to be resurrected, to be re-embodied in the everlasting 'matter' of the world to come. Where will that 'matter' come from? Surely it will be the transformed and glorified matter of the old creation, just as the Lord's risen and glorified body was the transmutation of his dead body. Our destiny and the destiny of the whole universe lie together. If you take resurrection and new creation seriously, you have to take the cosmic Christ seriously, who has 'the first place in everything'.

These are mysterious and exciting ideas. I can't pretend to understand all that they mean. The answer to many of our questions has to be 'wait and see'. I am convinced, however, that our thought and hope have to be as wide as this if Christian belief is to make any sense at all. It is a great mistake to be too spiritually minded. Christianity at its best and truest has always taken the whole of the created world seriously. Matter matters. That is why the empty tomb is important. In Christ there is a destiny for the material as well as the human. I shall return to that theme on Easter Day.

We have already warned ourselves not to make God too small. We must also beware of making Christ too small. He who humbled himself to accept the limitations of a first-century Jew, and the ultimate limitation of dying nailed to a cross, is the one who is the ruler and the hope of all the starry heavens.

PRAYER

Lord Jesus Christ, you are the redeemer of all that is, of space and time, stars and galaxies, matter and energy and consciousness. In you we place our hope, now and for ever.

SEARCHING

UNDERSTANDING

Proverbs 8:1–5

Does not wisdom call,
and does not understanding raise her voice?
On the heights, beside the way,
at the crossroads she takes her stand;
beside the gates in front of the town,
at the entrance of the portals she cries out:
'To you, O people, I call,
and my cry is to all that live.
O simple ones, learn prudence;
acquire intelligence, you who lack it.'

The desire to make sense of the world is a very deep human longing. The search for understanding is a great endeavour in which we should all be engaged. It is an activity which is natural to the scientist, for the wish to understand the physical world is the prime motive for all basic scientific research. Yet we have seen that the thirst for understanding will not be quenched by science alone. The latter achieves its great success by the modesty of its ambitions. It only asks certain restricted questions and it only considers certain limited, impersonal, forms of experience. Much of the highest value and significance eludes its grasp.

When I talked about natural theology, I suggested that it provided a way of seeking a deeper intelligibility, a more profound understanding of the many-layered reality within which we live. That is a step in the right direction, but we cannot stop there. It is necessary to press on in our search to take into account more particular and personal encounters. We need to know, not only what things are like, but how we should behave. The search for knowledge turns into the search for wisdom. This is symbolized for us by the book of Proverbs which depicts Wisdom, not as an encyclopaedia of facts, but as a person whose cry is to all that live.

In the eighteenth century a great intellectual movement began which scholars call the Enlightenment. Encouraged by the successes of scientific discovery, particularly the wonderful achievements of Sir Isaac Newton, people began to take dispassionate, detached scientific investigation as the model for all forms of search for understanding. Only the objective and impersonal could count as real knowledge. The world pictured by such thought was grey and lifeless. Subjective understanding was devalued and personal experience neglected. The so-called Enlightenment brought a kind of darkness of the spirit. There were those who protested, of course, particularly the poets and the artists. The whole Romantic movement, which we associate with people such as William Wordsworth and William Blake, was a reaction against such a diminished view of reality. They were right to protest. So bleak a world can have no real knowledge in it because there is no room within its narrow compass for the human knower.

Similar impoverished accounts of reality are offered to us today. There are people who will tell us that we are just genetic survival machines or that we are computers made of meat. We should reject these implausible and inadequate claims. Subjective knowledge and experience are as important as objective knowledge and experience. Only if we recognize that will we have the chance to find full understanding and to acquire wisdom.

PRAYER

*Lord, grant us wisdom and understanding that we
may know your truth and obey your will.*

THE WORD

J o h n   1 : 1 – 4 ,   1 4

In the beginning was the Word, and the Word was with God, and the Word was God. He was in the beginning with God. All things came into being through him, and without him not one thing came into being. What has come into being in him was life, and the life was the light of all people... And the Word became flesh and lived among us, and we have seen his glory, the glory as of a father's only son, full of grace and truth.

We are so used to hearing the famous prologue to St John's Gospel read at carol services that, perhaps, we let the familiar phrases flow over us. Let's stop and think for a minute about one of them: 'The Word'. In English, it is rather an odd way of speaking but in the ancient world it would have made sense, both to Greeks and to Hebrews.

The Greek word for 'word', *logos*, has a richer meaning that its English counterpart. One of its basic concepts is that of order, so that it stands for the reliable pattern and structure of the universe. A scientist full of wonder at one of the beautiful equations that describe this mathematical world, is rejoicing in the *logos*. In the Greek mind 'word' represented the harmony of being.

The Hebrews thought differently. Their language is one in which verbs play the leading role; they were a people for whom action and movement mattered. The Hebrew *dabar* has this sense of activity about it. It is the word of the Lord which came to the prophets in warning and judgment, the word of the Lord by which the heavens were made (Psalm 33:6). In the Hebrew mind 'word' represented God's activity in creation and in history.

I am sure that John is deliberately wanting to evoke both these meanings in the minds of his first readers. He is talking both about the divinely ordained order of the world and the divine activity within it. The One through whom all things came into being is the God of both being and becoming.

When the famous fourth-century thinker, St Augustine, who had been greatly influenced by the thought of Plato and his followers, came to read the prologue to St John's Gospel as part of his exploration of Christianity, he found much that was already familiar to him. Then he came across something which astonished him and for which Plato had not prepared him: 'The Word became flesh and lived among us.'

Here he encountered, and we encounter, the essential and exciting idea which lies at the heart of Christianity. In our search for understanding, we all long to know what is the ultimate answer. What is deepest reality actually like? What is God like? These seem to be questions which are too profound for our feeble human minds to answer. Yet God has acted to answer them for us. He has made himself known in the plainest and most accessible way, by living the life of man in Jesus Christ. Do you want to know what the God of being and becoming is really like, the One who sustains the order of the universe and whose providence is at work within its history? If you really want to know the answer, then look at Jesus Christ, the living and personal Word of God.

PRAYER

May we behold Christ's glory, the glory as of a father's only son, full of grace and truth. Illuminate our hearts and minds, Lord Jesus, with the light of your presence.

EXPERIENCE

1 John 1 : 1 - 3

*We declare to you what was from the beginning, what we
have heard, what we have seen with our eyes, what we
have looked at and touched with our hands, concerning
the word of life—this life was revealed, and we have seen
it and testify to it, and declare to you the eternal life that
was with the Father and was revealed to us—we declare
to you what we have seen and heard so that you also may
have fellowship with us; and truly our fellowship is with
the Father and with his Son Jesus Christ.*

Politicians sometimes use the world 'theological' as a term
of mild abuse. They apply it to an idea because they want
to suggest that there is really no reason for believing that it
corresponds to how things actually are. They think that
theology is something that is just spun out of the mind,
fantastic thoughts which have no basis in reality, concerned
with pseudo-problems, such as how many angels can dance
on the head of a pin. (Incidentally, friends who are experts
in medieval thought assure me that no one ever discussed
that particular speculative question.)

Those who use 'theological' in this sense display their
gross ignorance of what theology is like. They should all be
made to write out 1 John 1:1–3 a hundred times.

The writer is expounding the theme that we thought
about yesterday, the fundamental Christian idea that God
has made himself fully and explicitly known in Jesus

Christ. John's expression is very bold and direct. Those who knew Jesus in his earthly life had actually looked at and touched 'the word of life'. The hopeful paradox of the incarnation could not be put in blunter terms. The belief of the first Christians did not arise from idle thought or fanciful story-telling, but from personal encounter. Its origin was not in speculation but in experience.

But what about us, who live 2,000 years too late to have had that sort of meeting with Jesus? We shall encounter him in different ways.

One is through the Church, the Christian people we meet and respect and who influence our lives. Of course we all have friends whom we admire who are of different faiths or none. Yet I have to say that a very large proportion of the people whose integrity and wisdom and love I most greatly value—both among my personal acquaintance and among those in history whom I have learned about—are Christian believers. In the wholeness and openness of their lives I think I catch glimpses of the One we are all seeking to follow.

Another meeting point with Christ is the one that he himself instituted for us: the sacrament of the eucharist. There have been many unresolved arguments in the course of Christian history about how we are best able to understand the Lord's presence in the bread and wine of communion. It remains a mystery, but an experienced mystery. There has been great agreement among Christians that the Lord is to be met with in this special way, and I gladly add my own testimony to the real presence of Christ in the eucharist.

Yet another meeting point is the Lord's hidden presence in the poor and needy who cross our paths day by day. That is the point of the parable of the sheep and goats: 'Truly I tell you, just as you did it to one of the least of these who are members of my family, you did it to me' (Matthew 25:31–46).

Finally we meet the Lord in scripture. That is a subject which will concern us for the next few days.

P R A Y E R

Eternal God, you are the light of the minds that know you, the joy of the hearts that love you and the strength of the wills that serve you. Grant us so to know you that we may truly love you, and so to love you that we may fully serve you, whom to serve is perfect freedom.

St Augustine

SCRIPTURE

John 20:30-31; 21:24-25

*Now Jesus did many other signs in the presence of his
disciples, which are not written in this book. But these are
written so that you may come to believe that Jesus is the
Messiah, the Son of God, and that through believing you
may have life in his name... This is the disciple who is
testifying to these things and has written them, and we
know that his testimony is true. But there are also many
other things that Jesus did; if every one of them were
written down, I suppose that the world itself could not
contain the books that would be written.*

If we are to meet with Jesus, reading scripture will be an
especially important way of doing so. That will be particularly true, of course, of the Gospels, which are our main
sources of information about his life and death and resurrection.

In the verses I have quoted, John, and then, in the
second passage, probably someone else who knew the
main author of the Gospel, make plain the purpose of the
writing. It is 'that you may come to believe that Jesus is the
Messiah, the Son of God, and that through believing you
may have life in his name'. In other words, we are not
given some useful information on a 'take it or leave it'
basis. The Gospels are written to bring us life and to
change our lives. They are books with a purpose, and they
propose an interpretation of who Jesus was which will

affect us deeply if we come to accept it. The writers are selective. They cannot tell us all, but they concentrate on what is significant for their main purpose: the proclamation of the good news about Jesus Christ. In fact, they leave out a lot of things which those of us used to modern biographical style would rather like to know. For example, what did he look like?

It will come as no shock to a scientist to learn that the Gospels are selective and that they view what is happening in terms of a particular interpretative point of view. Experimental science does exactly the same. You cannot possibly look at everything that is going on in the physical world. That would be too bewildering. It is necessary to choose to look at what seem likely to be the illuminating events. That selection is what we mean by an experiment. The results of such an experiment will be measurements, numbers, graphs, but they will have no significance in themselves until we use scientific theory to give them a meaning. There are no interesting scientific facts which are not already *interpreted* facts.

In these respects the Gospel writers and modern scientists have important things in common. There is one further most necessary concern that they both share, which is to be true to what is happening, to tell it like it is. To be sure, there are disagreements and discrepancies among the Gospel writers (just exactly who were the women who discovered the empty tomb and at exactly what stage of the early morning did they do so?). Anyone who has listened to different witnesses describing the same incident will not be surprised at that. But we also have good reason to trust that they are, within the narrative conventions of the ancient world, seeking to give an honest account of what happened. They tell us embarrassing things which it would have been easier to have suppressed: that Peter denied Christ and that Jesus made the shocking remark, 'Let the dead bury their own dead' (Matthew 8:22). Only someone with a real concern for truth would have kept those incidents in their account.

We can trust the Gospel writers and we need to use their reliable record to help us to get to know the Jesus who had transformed their lives and who can transform ours.

P R A Y E R

Lord God, whose Word and will were made known in Jesus Christ, help us to meet him in the pages of holy scripture and to find life in his name.

LORD

Psalm 110:1-4

The Lord says to my lord,
  'Sit at my right hand
until I make your enemies your footstool.'
The Lord sends out from Zion
  your mighty sceptre.
  Rule in the midst of your foes.
Your people will offer themselves willingly
  on the day you lead your forces
  on the holy mountains.
From the womb of the morning,
  like dew, your youth will come to you.
The Lord has sworn and will not change his mind,
  'You are a priest for ever
  according to the order of Melchizedek.'

From the very first, Christians struggled to find ways of understanding their experience of Jesus. The new life he brought to them was of such quality that it did not seem possible adequately to describe him using human language alone. He was more than an inspiring teacher or the example of a good life. The earliest Christian confession seems to have been 'Jesus is Lord' (see 1 Corinthians 12:3). In first-century Palestine that was a more highly charged confession than we may at first sight realize today. Pious Jews never uttered aloud the name of God (*Yahweh*), but said instead 'Lord'. Therefore Jesus was being given a title with strong divine overtones. Yet he was being given it by Jews, whose central belief was that 'the Lord our God is one Lord' (Deuteronomy 6:4). How then could Jesus be Lord too? In their struggle to make sense of this paradox, forced on them by experience, the first Christians searched their scriptures, the Old Testament, for clues. One of the ones they came upon was the opening verses of Psalm 110. It is, in fact, the passage from the Old Testament which is most frequently quoted in the New Testament.

It pictures a Lordly figure sitting at the right hand of God, very much like the vision that the first martyr, Stephen, had of Jesus, just before he was stoned to death (Acts 7:55–56). Jesus is God's right-hand man, so to speak. With hindsight we can see that this picture, though it was helpful, did not resolve all questions about how Christ and God are related to each other. Eventually, after much thought, the Church found that the only way adequately to understand the nature of Jesus was to believe that God was truly living a human life in him, though he was not identical with God, pure and simple. (They remembered how often Jesus had prayed to his heavenly Father, so that there was a distinction to be maintained between the two.) The end of their searching was the strange and exciting Christian idea of the incarnation.

Those early Christians believed that Jesus was Lord because they had found in their own lives that he was so. Then they used scripture to help them interpret their experience. In so doing they made the psalm carry a different meaning from that which it had when it was first written. Then it had been for use as a psalm at the enthronement of a king of Judah, understood as God's right-hand man, not in heaven but on earth. Psalm 110 found a new, but entirely legitimate, meaning when it was applied to the exalted Christ. Scripture is powerful and flexible, capable of carrying a number of meanings and not restricted solely to its original context.

A similar discovery of deeper meaning happened also for the fourth verse of the psalm. It refers to Melchizedek, the mysterious priest-king of Jerusalem, to whom Abraham (no less) paid tribute (Genesis 14:17–20). Here was another powerful symbol which could be used to help understand the exalted status of Christ. The epistle to the Hebrews can be seen as an extended meditation on the insights which derive from thinking of our Lord Jesus Christ in the light of Psalm 110.

P R A Y E R

Son of God, our Saviour, may we confess you as our Lord and may you rule in our hearts as you rule in heaven.

A UNIVERSITY SERMON

Acts 17:22–23, 26–28, 30–31

*Then Paul stood in front of the Areopagus and said,
'Athenians, I see how extremely religious you are in every
way. For as I went through the city and looked carefully
at the objects of your worship, I found among them an
altar with the inscription, "To an unknown god." What
therefore you worship as unknown, this I proclaim to
you... From one ancestor he made all nations to inhabit
the whole earth, and he allotted the times of their existence
and the boundaries of the places where they would live, so
that they would search for God and perhaps grope for him
and find him—though indeed he is not far from each one
of us. For "In him we live and move and have our
being"; as even some of your own poets have said, "For
we too are his offspring."... While God has overlooked the
times of human ignorance, now he commands all people
everywhere to repent, because he has fixed a day on which
he will have the world judged in righteousness by a man
whom he has appointed, and of this he has given
assurance to all by raising him from the dead.'*

The Greeks loved to talk and the Athenians were the most
talkative of the lot. They had their meeting place for
discussion, the Areopagus, a kind of intellectual Hyde Park
Corner. There they persuaded St Paul to tell them all
about his new ideas. I suppose that you could call it his
University Sermon.

Paul starts where they are, first referring to the altar he had seen dedicated 'To an unknown God'. This was a kind of hedging of religious bets. Just in case there was some deity whom they had forgotten and who might be offended at being overlooked, the Athenians tried to cover themselves by having this spare altar that could be allocated to the neglected god. We are all anxious about ultimate reality. What is it really like? Is it on our side? Paul tells the Athenians that the true God has acted to make himself known.

Paul knows that his hearers are concerned about religious matters. They have their poets who have spoken about the divine presence in which 'we live and move and have our being'. Paul does not despise Greek religion but he knows that it is not enough. We are surrounded in this country by people who have some sort of religious feelings and concern. Opinion polls reveal that a large majority of people in Britain believe in some sort of God, far more people than ever go to a place of worship. This kind of submerged belief in an almost unknown god is sometimes called 'folk religion'. We are not to despise it, though by itself it is not enough.

Paul goes on to speak to the Athenians about Jesus and his resurrection. The reaction is mixed. Some find this too much to take on board; others want to hear more about it; eventually there are some who embrace the faith of Christ.

Paul starts where his hearers are and he ends with Jesus Christ. That is the way that all evangelists have to set about proclaiming the Christian gospel. We have to respect and understand the position and experiences of those we meet; we have also to testify to the risen Lord. Not many of us are called to preach University Sermons, or indeed sermons of any kind. But all Christian people are called, humbly, tactfully, respectfully, firmly, to be witnesses to Jesus Christ as opportunity and circumstances permit. If we are willing and open, there is no doubt that such occasions will come our way.

PRAYER

Father, help us to testify to the truth revealed in your Son, Jesus Christ. May the Spirit guide us, that with our lives and with our lips we may witness to the risen Lord.

SOME DOUBTED

Matthew 28:16–20

*Now the eleven disciples went to Galilee, to the mountain
to which Jesus had directed them. When they saw him,
they worshipped him; but some doubted. And Jesus came
and said to them, 'All authority in heaven and on earth
has been given to me. Go therefore and make disciples of
all nations, baptizing them in the name of the Father and
of the Son and of the Holy Spirit, and teaching them to
obey everything that I have commanded you. And
remember, I am with you always, to the end of the age.'*

Matthew ends his Gospel with a final appearance of the
risen Christ, who proclaims that all power is in his Lordly
hands and that he will be with us as long as the world lasts.
It is a scene of great triumph, but Matthew tells us that
when Jesus appeared on that mountain in Galilee, though
many worshipped him, 'some doubted'.

I want to say two things about that. One is to notice that
here we have another example of how the Gospel writers
are trying honestly to tell it like it was and not to gloss over
unpalatable facts.

The second thing is to point out that this difficulty in
recognizing the risen Christ, of being sure at first that it
was actually him, is a theme that recurs in the stories of the
resurrection appearances. Each Gospel has its own account
of various occasions on which Jesus showed himself after
his resurrection and it is not altogether easy to see exactly

how they all fit together. Yet in many of them we find, in one way or another, this problem of recognition.

Mary Magdalene mistakes Jesus for the gardener and asks him where he has removed the body. Only when the Lord speaks her name does Mary realize who it is that she has encountered (John 20:14–16). The two on the road to Emmaus only realize right at the end who the stranger is who has been talking to them (Luke 24:13–32). When Jesus appears to the disciples gathered in Jerusalem, at first they don't know what to make of it and fear that they are seeing a ghost (Luke 24:36–40). In the light of early morning, only the beloved disciple among the fishing party has the insight to recognize the figure standing on the shore of the Lake of Galilee (John 21:4–7).

Eventually Jesus was recognizable—his body still carried the scars of the passion—but not necessarily at first sight. There was both continuity and discontinuity between the earthly Jesus and the risen Jesus, which could inhibit immediate recognition.

This persistent theme of initial uncertainty about who it was is expressed in differing ways in the various stories of the appearances. It seems a most unlikely detail to have been made up independently by several different writers. I think it is the sign of a genuine historical reminiscence about the appearance of the risen Lord. Some may have doubted, but for us their very difficulty can come as an assurance that the stories we are reading were based on actual experience.

PRAYER

Lord, help us to recognize you as we meet you in our daily lives, particularly in the poor and needy who cross our paths. May your hidden presence be with us all, till the end of the age.

PRAYER

ASKING

Matthew 7 : 7 – 11

*'Ask, and it will be given you; search, and you will
find; knock, and the door will be opened for you. For
everyone who asks receives, and everyone who searches
finds, and for everyone who knocks, the door will be
opened. Is there anyone among you who, if your child
asks for bread, will give a stone? Or if the child asks for
a fish, will give a snake? If you then, who are evil, know
how to give good gifts to your children, how much more
will your Father in heaven give good things to those who
ask him!'*

In this passage from the Sermon on the Mount, Jesus
encourages us, in the most direct way possible, to ask God
for things. We may feel some embarrassment at the blunt
way in which it is put: 'Ask, and it will be given you.' Do we
really believe that?

I think we feel a number of difficulties. One of them
certainly arises from modern science. Isn't the world so
regular and orderly that things just *happen*, whatever we
(or even God?) try to do about it? In the *Book of Common
Prayer* of 1662 there is a petition asking for seasonable
weather. When the prayer book was revised in 1928, that
kind of prayer was retained, but you will search the 1980
Alternative Service Book in vain for its contemporary counterpart. The nearest you will get is a harvest collect
giving thanks afterwards for the fruits of the earth. It's

not entirely clear why we should be thankful after the event for what we did not have the nerve to ask for beforehand!

Many congregations would feel uneasy about praying for rain. Won't the weather just be what it's going to be? Well, remember the butterfly effect (page 52)? It's all a bit more subtle than a merely mechanical unfolding of the inevitable. The physical world seems to have an openness to the future about it, which is no doubt how we are able to act in a free and responsible way within it. If that's the case for us, why shouldn't it be so for God as well? I don't think that the effect of purely physical causes is drawn so tightly that it rules out either human choice or divine providence.

But isn't there a second difficulty, namely that just asking God for things is surely a pretty childish way of praying? Of course, it's not the only way to pray—there's praise, and confession and meditation—but it's one way and we see that it's a way that Jesus strongly endorses. Rather than being childish, it is childlike—a different attitude altogether and one highly recommended in the Gospels (see Matthew 18:3). We believe in a personal God, and that must mean a God who does particular things for particular people in particular circumstances. He is not a 'force' like gravity, always the same, but a Father who will 'give good things to those that ask him'.

Are we, then, given a book of blank cheques, drawn on the account of a kind of heavenly Father Christmas, that we can fill in and use just as we like? What happens when the farmer prays for rain for the crops and the vicar prays for a dry day for the church fête? Who wins? Petitionary prayer is real, but it is not as crudely mechanical as that. What this means will be something we shall have to think about together this week.

PRAYER

Heavenly Father, we thank you that you care for us, your children. Give us a prayerful trust and confidence in your goodness.

FELLOW WORKERS

2 Corinthians 6:1; Philippians 2:12–13

As we work together with him, we urge you also not to accept the grace of God in vain...

Therefore, my beloved, just as you have always obeyed me, not only in my presence, but much more now in my absence, work out your own salvation with fear and trembling; for it is God who is at work in you, enabling you both to will and to work for his good pleasure.

Why do we have to ask at all? Children don't usually need continually to persuade their parents to look after them. If God is really good and really cares for us, why doesn't he just get on with it? What are we doing when we pray?

Are we making such a fuss that God just has to take notice of us? Are we drawing his attention to something he might otherwise have forgotten? Or suggesting a cunning plan he might not otherwise have thought of? Obviously, none of these things can possibly be what prayer is about. So what is going on?

I think there are two important things happening when we prayerfully ask God for something. One I will talk about today, the other tomorrow. Today's theme is that in prayer we offer ourselves to become fellow workers with God. We have been given some power to bring things about. God has also retained some providential power to bring things about. Prayer is seeking the alignment of our possibilities for action with God's possibility for action. In more traditional language, we offer our wills to be taken by God and used to the maximum effect in fulfilling his will. That is why all prayer has an implicit clause 'if it is your will'—not because we are trying to give God a let-out if it doesn't happen, but to indicate what it is we really ought to be seeking.

When human and divine wills are aligned in this way, I believe that things become possible which would be impossible if they were at cross purposes with each other. An analogy I like is taken from physics. We all know that laser light has all sorts of remarkable and unusual properties. That is because it is what the physicists call 'coherent'; all its waves are in step. Crest coincides with crest, trough with trough. There is no mutual cancellation and so you get the maximum effect. In incoherent light, a crest and a trough can coincide and cancel each other out. What we are seeking in prayer is a laser-like coherence of divine and human will.

Two things follow from this. One is that prayer is a spur to action and not a substitute for it. If my young neighbour is harassed by the need to cope with her over-active young children, I cannot truly pray for her without also being willing to help her in some way if I can.

The second thing is that it explains something that we all believe, namely that it is good to have many people praying for the same thing. This is not because we'll then make more noise and be more likely to attract God's attention. It's because there are then more wills available to cooperate with the divine will. In petitionary prayer we are offered the privilege of becoming fellow workers with God.

PRAYER

Father, you have given us the precious gift of prayer. Help us use it to offer our lives and will to you for the fulfilment of your purposes of love in the world.

WHAT DO YOU WANT?

Luke 18:35–43

As he approached Jericho, a blind man was sitting by the roadside begging. When he heard a crowd going by, he asked what was happening. They told him, 'Jesus of Nazareth is passing by.' Then he shouted, 'Jesus, Son of David, have mercy on me!' Those who were in front sternly ordered him to be quiet; but he shouted even more loudly. 'Son of David, have mercy on me!' Jesus stood still and ordered the man to be brought to him; and when he came near, he asked him, 'What do you want me to do for you?' He said, 'Lord, let me see again.' Jesus said to him, 'Receive your sight; your faith has saved you.' Immediately he regained his sight and followed him, glorifying God; and all the people, when they saw it praised God.

The blind man succeeds in attracting Jesus' attention. He makes his way to the front of the crowd and stands before the Lord. Jesus says to him, 'What do you want me to do for you?' Isn't it obvious? He's a *blind* man, for goodness sake. He wants his sight. Yet he has to say to Jesus, 'Lord, let me see again' before he is healed. The blind man has to commit himself by the act of a definite asking.

This story illustrates the second thing that I think we are doing when we pray. We are saying what it is we really want, what is our heart's desire. We are called upon to assign value, to commit ourselves to what comes first in our lives. God will take that seriously. I've already said that prayer is not just a case of filling out a blank cheque with anything that lightly takes our fancy. But if we really want it, seriously, committedly, carefully, then God will receive that as our true request.

I find this a helpful and a sobering thought about prayer. Remember, we are asking in the presence of God. We may well get what we request. Certainly what we receive will be related to what we have asked for. Prayer is a serious business.

So what do we want above all else? Success? Comfort? Affection? Respect? Health? All these things are good and if we are anxious about them, we should certainly express our concerns to God. But what is the deepest of our desires?

I often think how transformed our lives would be if we really, deep down within us, fully believed that God loves us. If our trust was full and steadfast, rather than feeble and perhaps fleeting, what different people we should be. I think that is my heart's desire, to know the love of God. One of my favourite verses from the Psalms, which I often use as a little arrow prayer, is:

'Come', my heart says, 'seek his face!'
Your face, Lord, do I seek.

Psalm 27:8

What do you want?

P R A Y E R

Lord, may we come to know you, the only true God,
and Jesus Christ whom you have sent.

HONESTY

Psalm 42:9–10

I say to God, my rock,
  'Why have you forgotten me?
Why must I walk about mournfully
  because the enemy oppresses me?'
As with a deadly wound in my body,
  my adversaries taunt me,
while they say to me continually,
  'Where is your God?'

When we pray we are in the presence of the God 'to whom all hearts are open, all desires known, and from whom no secrets are hidden'. Before this God there is neither room nor need for any pretence. We do not have to keep up pious appearances. The God of truth expects us to be absolutely honest with him.

There will be times when we come to pray when we shall be weary, bitter, perplexed, resentful. The way to deal with these feelings is not to cover them up in some pitiful attempt to put a brave spiritual face on it. We can express them and lay them before the Lord. Only if our hearts are exposed can they be healed. We do not need to fear that God will be shocked. That includes the expression of anger at him in the face of some tragic disaster.

The Psalmists greatly encourage us by the example of their honesty. Today's reading portrays someone in great trouble who fears that he or she has been forgotten by God and who is bold enough to say so. There are many such passages in the Psalms.

Why, O Lord, do you stand far off?
Why do you hide yourself in times of trouble?

Psalm 10:1

Praying in this way is painful but it is also truthful. Part of our life of prayer will be the stripping off of all the layers of pretence by which we insulate ourselves from reality.

We, all of us, carry hidden hurts and anxieties which, if we can share them at all, we only dare to do occasionally and with someone whom we trust very profoundly. God is always there for us if we will turn to him. And remember, he knows human life from the inside, because he has lived a human life in Jesus Christ.

One of the saddest situations one can encounter is one in which there is a conspiracy of unreality. Perhaps someone is dying, and the family have decided not to acknowledge the fact openly for the sake, as they see it, of the person involved. Very frequently that person is aware of their situation but doesn't want to upset the family by making this clear. Best intentions are involved on both sides, but the denial of reality can often produce an atmosphere which frustrates the possibility of mutual comfort and farewell in the precious time remaining.

God is ultimate Reality and he can accept us as we are. Honesty is an indispensable quality in prayer.

P R A Y E R

Lord, so assure us of your steadfast love, that
we may dare to speak to you in honesty and
sincerity from the mixed feelings of our hearts.

THE THORN IN THE FLESH

2 Corinthians 12:7–10

Therefore, to keep me from being too elated, a thorn was given me in the flesh, a messenger of Satan to torment me, to keep me from being too elated. Three times I appealed to the Lord about this, that it would leave me, but he said to me, 'My grace is sufficient for you, for power is made perfect in weakness.' So, I will boast all the more gladly of my weaknesses, so that the power of Christ may dwell in me. Therefore I am content with weaknesses, insults, hardships, persecutions, and calamities for the sake of Christ; for whenever I am weak, then I am strong.

I suppose that one of the other difficulties which many people feel about petitionary prayer is that so often it doesn't actually seem to work. There is so much that God might do, from curing our young neighbour who has liver cancer to bringing peace to a war-torn country, but which doesn't actually come about. No one can talk about prayer with any honesty without facing the mystery of individual destiny. In our passage today we find St Paul doing just that on his own account.

He had some serious disability from which he earnestly sought to be made free. He calls it his thorn in the flesh. Scholars have speculated what it might have been but we don't really know. No doubt it impeded Paul in his great task of bringing the good news of Jesus Christ to the

Gentiles. Surely, God ought to do something to take it away? Eventually Paul receives a definite answer. It is his destiny to have to live with this particular weakness. It is something to be accepted and not removed.

God's grace will be sufficient, but that could not have been an easy message for Paul to receive. When we face some profound problem, in our life or in the life of someone close to us, we all long for some stroke of magic which will take it away and make everything right again, just as it used to be. Prayer is not that sort of magical lever which we can use in this way. God is a God of steadfast love, but he is not a magician. Tomorrow, when we think of Gethsemane, we shall see what that meant for God's own Son.

Someone is very ill. That person's Christian friends will pray for healing, that is to say, wholeness. No one can say beforehand whether that wholeness will come from physical recovery or from accepting the imminent destiny of death. The evangelist, David Watson, must have been one of the people most earnestly prayed for when it was discovered that he had cancer. He began to write what was to be his last book, *Fear No Evil*. One feels that he did so expecting that it would record a miraculous story of a malignancy cured. In fact, as you read it, you share in a miraculous story of the approach of death acknowledged and accepted in the peace of Christ.

Although the form of a prayed-for wholeness cannot be laid down beforehand, the sustaining reality of prayer can certainly be experienced. Some years ago, when I was a middle-aged curate in Bristol, suddenly and unexpectedly I became seriously ill. My life was diminished and reduced to the narrow confines of my hospital bed and the drips which were keeping me alive. God seemed very far away, but I was conscious of being prayed for and much upheld by that knowledge. Prayer is not magic but it is certainly real.

P R A Y E R

Lord, may your grace be sufficient for me, may your power be made perfect in my weakness.

GETHSEMANE

Mark 14:32-42

They went to a place called Gethsemane; and he said to his disciples, 'Sit here while I pray.' He took with him Peter and James and John, and began to be distressed and agitated. And said to them, 'I am deeply grieved, even to death; remain here, and keep awake.' And going a little farther, he threw himself on the ground and prayed that, if it were possible, the hour might pass from him. He said, 'Abba, Father, for you all things are possible; remove this cup from me; yet, not what I want, but what you want.' He came and found them sleeping; and he said to Peter, 'Simon, are you asleep? Could you not keep awake one hour? Keep awake and pray that you may not come into the time of trial; the spirit indeed is willing, but the flesh is weak.' And again he went away and prayed, saying the same words. And once more he came and found them sleeping, for their eyes were very heavy; and they did not know what to say to him. He came a third time and said to them, 'Are you still sleeping and taking your rest? Enough! The hour has come; the Son of Man is betrayed into the hands of sinners. Get up, let us be going. See, my betrayer is at hand.'

Gethsemane is one of the most profound and holy scenes in the whole Gospel story.

Jesus came to Jerusalem knowing that his final confrontation with the authorities could no longer be delayed, expecting to be put to death, and trusting that God would vindicate him. He accepted his destiny with total commitment, but that did not mean that it became easy or costless for him. The scene in the garden makes it clear just how great was the cost of our redemption.

Jesus becomes distressed and agitated. He prays to God using the intimate word 'Abba', that a trusting child would use to a trusted parent. He asks that the cup of suffering should be taken away from him, 'yet not what I want, but what you want'. The cup was not removed. Even as the disciples fitfully and fearfully dozed, the betrayer was on his way to hand Jesus over to trial and execution.

It is a conventionally unheroic scene. Jesus seems to face death with less calm and self-possession than Socrates had shown, or than many Christian martyrs were later to display. We have to ask: what was going on?

One of the Greek Fathers of the Church said that Christ shared our humanity so that we might share in his divinity. Jesus shared human experience fully, truly and to the uttermost. Another of the Fathers, Gregory of Nazianzus, said that what was not assumed would not be healed. In other words, it is precisely because Jesus accepted all of human experience, and was not insulated from any of the blows that life can bring, that he is able to bring us redemption and new life.

In Gethsemane we see what this total identification of Christ with the human condition meant for Jesus. He assumes, and fully shares, the natural human dread of nothingness which comes upon us in the face of death. It was because he did this that death did not have the last word for him, nor will it have for us. What was assumed has truly and finally been healed.

The writer of the epistle to the Hebrews refers to Gethsemane when he says that 'In the days of his flesh, Jesus offered up prayers and supplications, with loud cries and tears, to the one who was able to save him from death,

and he was heard because of his reverent submission'
(Hebrews 5:7). The way that Jesus' prayer was heard was
that he was strengthened to accept the destiny of his death
on the cross.

P R A Y E R

By your agony and trial; by your cross and passion;
by your precious death and burial, Good Lord,
deliver us.

ASB, Litany

CRUCIFIXION

Mark 15:22–28

Then they brought Jesus to the place called Golgotha (which means the place of a skull). And they offered him wine mixed with myrrh; but he did not take it. And they crucified him, and divided his clothes among them, casting lots to decide what each should take. It was nine o'clock in the morning when they crucified him. The inscription of the charge against him read, 'The King of the Jews.' And with him they crucified two bandits, one on his right and one on his left.

Crucifixion was a prolonged and painful death. It had been devised deliberately as an act of deadly torture. There was the pain of the wounds, the exposure to heat and flies, the thirst, the mocking by spectators. Above all, there was the continual struggle to breathe. Each laborious breath could only be made by the crucified forcing himself to the agonizing act of lifting himself on the cross to gasp another lungful of air. Eventually the struggle failed and death came through asphyxiation. Often this could take more than a day to happen but it was possible to shorten the ordeal by breaking the legs of the crucified so that he was no longer able to make the movement necessary to gain the next breath.

Crucifixion was a shameful death. Because of its horrible character, it was reserved for slaves and felons, the lowest of the low.

For a Jew, crucifixion was a God-forsaken death. 'Cursed is everyone who hangs on a tree', wrote St Paul (Galatians 3:13), looking back to a verse in Deuteronomy. It must have seemed the absolute denial of all the disciples' hopes that Jesus was God's chosen Messiah, when they saw that he was to be put to death in this way.

It is difficult for us to recover the feeling of horror that a word like 'cross' evoked in the ancient world. It was not an ecclesiastical symbol, as it is for us today, but a ghastly gallows. The use of the cross in Christian art comes very late, about a century after the abolition of this form of execution, when the memory of its horror had had time to fade.

Yet for Christians, the tree of shame is the tree of glory. Christ is the king who reigns from the gallows. Three times in St John's Gospel there is a grim pun about the Son of Man being 'lifted up' (John 3:14; 8:28; 12:32–34). At one level it is a clear reference to death by crucifixion, just as, in the days of hanging, people spoke of someone being 'topped'. But for John, who delights in the divine irony of the incarnation, the lifting up of Jesus on the cross is also the moment of his true exaltation. 'And I, when I am lifted up from the earth, will draw all people to myself' (John 12:32). As the passion approaches, Jesus says 'The hour has come for the Son of Man to be glorified' (John 12:23).

P R A Y E R

Thanks be to you, my Lord Jesus Christ, for all the benefits you have won for me, for all the pains and insults you have borne for me. O most merciful Redeemer, Friend and Brother, may I know you more clearly, love you more dearly, and follow you more nearly, day by day.

Richard of Chichester

SUFFERING

NATURAL DISASTER

Psalm 29:3-9

The voice of the Lord is over the waters;
the God of glory thunders,
the Lord, over mighty waters.
The voice of the Lord is powerful;
the voice of the Lord is full of majesty
The voice of the Lord breaks the cedars;
the Lord breaks the cedars of Lebanon.
He makes Lebanon skip like a calf,
and Sirion like a young wild ox.
The voice of the Lord flashes forth flames of fire.
The voice of the Lord shakes the wilderness;
the Lord shakes the wilderness of Kadesh.
The voice of the Lord causes the oaks to whirl,
and strips the forest bare;
and in his temple all say, 'Glory!'

Psalm 29 describes a violent storm sweeping over the eastern seaboard of the Mediterranean. It brings with it great destruction, but for the Psalmist it serves as a sign of God's mighty power. 'In his temple all say, "Glory!"'

We are likely to view such an occurrence in a rather different way. Its destructiveness will present a problem for us, rather than its being the occasion for rejoicing. The issue of suffering in the world is one of the great perplexities with which theology has to wrestle. Natural disasters are part of that problem. The world does not look at first sight like the creation of a benevolent and almighty God. I think this is the greatest difficulty which holds people back from religious belief, and those of us who are believers can never be unconscious of its challenge.

In 1755 there was a great earthquake in Lisbon on 1 November, All Saints' Day. The churches were all full. Most collapsed and 50,000 people died. What was God doing in the Lisbon earthquake? I think that the answer is that he was allowing the earth's crust to behave in accordance with its nature. That may seem a hard, even callous, response, but I believe it is the truth. We have thought that in creation God has brought into being a world which he allows to be itself and to make itself. The gift of divine love has been to bestow this independence on the creation. God is neither a tyrant nor a magician. That is why he allowed a tectonic plate to slip in 1755. That is why natural disasters are permitted to happen.

The biochemists tell us that exactly the same processes in cells which enable some to mutate and bring about new possibilities for life—in other words, the very source of the fruitful history of life on earth which eventually produced human beings—these same processes will enable other cells to mutate and become malignant. You cannot have one without the other. In other words, the cost of an evolving creation is that it contains the possibility of cancer. The physical evil that cancer represents is not there because God is indifferent or incompetent but because it is inescapable in a world that is making itself. I do not believe that God wills that anyone should suffer from a malignant disease, but he allows that to happen in a world which is not his puppet theatre.

I do not for a moment pretend that these insights remove the profound and problematic mystery of human suffering. It is too deep a question to be disposed of in this intellectual way alone. I do think, however, that these insights are mildly helpful, in that they show that the existence of natural disaster is not a gratuitous oversight but the necessary cost of a free creation.

P R A Y E R

Father, we pray for all those who suffer from natural disasters: disease, famine, destruction. Make us mindful of their needs and give them your support in their adversity.

HONEST EXPRESSION

Psalm 69:1-3

Save me, O God,
  for the waters have come up to my neck.
I sink in deep mire,
  where there is no foothold;
I have come into deep waters,
  and the flood sweeps over me.
I am weary with my crying;
  my throat is parched.
My eyes grow dim
  with waiting for my God.

These moving words come from someone who is in great distress. For verse after verse following on those quoted, the Psalmist speaks of all the insults and enmity coming upon him. Nothing is held back or glossed over. Once again, we see the honesty of the writer in his dealings with God.

Suffering shared is suffering that is easier to bear. Loneliness and isolation only intensify the pain. Often we find it hard to expose our deepest sufferings to other people. Our feelings of vulnerability hold us back. Yet, often we are unable fully to acknowledge to ourselves what is going on without the help of someone to share it with us. God may well send us help through our family or friends, but it is also possible to approach him directly and honestly, as the Psalmist does in today's passage.

In the Christian use of the Psalms, these words of

121

Psalm 69 are frequently associated with the passion of Christ. That reminds us that in Christ God has come to know human suffering from the inside. To use some words of A.N. Whitehead, he is 'the fellow sufferer who understands'.

There is no doubt that common experience is a powerful basis for supportive sharing. When I was a parochial clergyman, I naturally did a fair amount of hospital visiting. I tried to be sympathetic and comforting to those I met in this way. Frequently that meant just being with that person, rather than having some wonderfully helpful thing that you could say to them. Then I had the experience of being seriously ill myself and in particular I went through the painful aftermath of abdominal surgery. Subsequently, if I visited people who were going through the same experience, I could truly tell them that I knew what it was like and they could recognize in me a fellow sufferer who understood. I had not learned some wonderfully helpful new thing to say, but my being with them now had a quality of sharing which was of value.

Christ can be alongside all of us in that special way. There is a method of praying which some people find helpful. It is to imagine that Jesus is sitting in the chair opposite and just to talk to him, telling him about our state and what is on our mind. That is one way in which we can follow the Psalmist's example of honest expression. We can trust that Christ will understand.

P R A Y E R

Lord Jesus, you know the bitterness that human
life can sometimes bring. Be with all in great
distress and help them to know your
compassionate friendship.

WORSHIP AND PERPLEXITY

Psalm 73:13-17

All in vain I have kept my heart clean
and washed my hands in innocence.
For all day long I have been plagued,
and am punished every morning.
If I had said, 'I will talk on in this way,'
I would have been untrue to the circle of your
children.
But when I thought how to understand this,
it seemed to me a wearisome task,
until I went into the sanctuary of God;
then I perceived their end.

We are perplexed and troubled when bad things happen to good people. In the Old Testament, the writers are equally dismayed when good things happen to bad people. The prosperity of the wicked is a real problem for them.

Psalm 73 is a kind of miniature book of Job, in which the Psalmist wrestles with this perplexity. At first, he is inclined to think that the wicked have it so good ('For they have no pain; their bodies are sound and sleek'; v. 4) that it is a waste of time to try to follow a good life. Today's passage tells us how he came to see that this view was a bad mistake. It was in the temple, the sanctuary of God, that he saw that the apparent triumph of evil is only temporary. God alone lasts for ever and it is his righteousness which will prevail.

It was the experience of worship which helped the Psalmist to resolve his perplexity.

Worship, of course, means acknowledging worth when it is present. It is seeing things as they really are—above all, God as he really is. People sometimes think of the worshipping Christian community as being a holy huddle, in flight from reality and living in a world of fantasy. The very reverse is the case for true worship. We go to church on Sunday, not to get another dose of spiritual anaesthetic to carry us through the coming week, but to regain our contact with things as they are. Worship involves a clearing of the eyes of the spirit. You will find that people who live a life of regular worship, even if it is pursued in a setting of monastic seclusion, are among the most open to reality that you can find. If you have the good habit of making an annual retreat—spending a few days in prayer and meditation and silence—it will help you to remain in contact with the deepest truth.

Superficial experience presses in on us all the time. We must not allow it to dominate our view. Saint Paul saw this very clearly. He wrote to the Corinthians: 'So we do not lose heart. Even though our outer nature is wasting away, our inner nature is being renewed day by day. For this slight momentary affliction is preparing us for an eternal weight of glory beyond all measure, because we look not at what can be seen but at what cannot be seen; for what can be seen is temporary, but what cannot be seen is eternal' (2 Corinthians 4:16–18).

PRAYER

*Lord God, the protector of all who trust in you,
without whom nothing is strong, nothing is holy:
increase and multiply upon us your mercy, that you
being our ruler and guide, we may so pass through
things temporal that we finally lose not the things
eternal. Grant this, heavenly Father, for the sake of
Jesus Christ our Lord.*

ASB, collect for Pentecost 14

THE APOSTOLIC LIFE

2 Corinthians 6:4-10

*As servants of God we have commended ourselves in
every way: through great endurance, in afflictions,
hardships, calamities, beatings, imprisonments, riots,
labours, sleepless nights, hunger; by purity, knowledge,
patience, kindness, holiness of spirit, genuine love,
truthful speech, and the power of God; with the weapons
of righteousness for the right hand and for the left; in
honour and dishonour, in ill repute and good repute. We
are treated as impostors, and yet are true; as unknown,
and yet are well known; as dying, and see—we are alive;
as punished, and yet not killed; as sorrowful, yet always
rejoicing; as poor, yet making many rich; as having
nothing, and yet possessing everything.*

In paintings of the worship of heaven, the apostles are
there, in the front row of the throng around the central
glory of the Holy Trinity. On the west front of Wells
Cathedral, there they are again in the position of honour,
lined up just below Christ himself. No doubt these images
validly represent the eternal invisible status of the Lord's
chosen messengers of the gospel. Their historical, visible
lives, however, seemed very different.

St Paul, speaking from experience, describes the apos-
tolic life as one of 'afflictions, hardships, calamities...'.
Earlier in the Corinthian correspondence he had said, 'I
think that God has exhibited us apostles as last of all, as

though sentenced to death, because we have become a spectacle to the world, to angels and to mortals' (1 Corinthians 4:9). The image is drawn from the bloody proceedings of the arena, where men condemned to die were brought on stage at the end of the circus to suffer certain death in combat either with each other, or with professional gladiators, or with the wild beasts.

So which is it, glory or misery? It is both, in the irony of how the invisible and the visible relate to each other. The apostles are like those who are dying, but know they are alive, sorrowful yet always rejoicing.

Part of the mystery of suffering is the great variety of different effects it has upon different people. All of us experience to some degree the affliction that suffering brings, the pain and sorrow it inflicts. Yet for some this will result in diminishment and the stunting of their lives, whilst others will show such patience and victory over their negative experience that it seems that a greater good is flowering from the seed of the evil that has come upon them. It is part of the enigma of suffering that there are these diverse individual responses to it. We do not know why the grace of God appears to act in so partial a way, but I am sure that we are right to see his Spirit at work in those who find light in their darkness.

It is deeply moving to be told that many Jews in the Nazi concentration camps were able to utter that great proclamation of faith, 'Hear, O Israel, the Lord our God is one Lord', even as they were being herded into the gas chambers.

Peter and Margaret Spufford had a dearly loved daughter, Bridget, who died aged twenty, after much suffering, from a congenital kidney disease. Despite the continuing pain of this tragic history, when Margaret came to write a book about the family's experience she was able to call her deep and moving account *Celebration* (Collins, 1989).

PRAYER

Almighty and everlasting God, the comfort of the sad, the strength of those who suffer: Let the prayers of your children who cry out of any tribulation come to you; and to every soul that is distressed grant mercy, relief and refreshment; through Jesus Christ our Lord.

The Gelasian Sacramentary

CRUCIFORM WISDOM

1 Corinthians 1:22-25

For Jews demand signs and Greeks desire wisdom, but we proclaim Christ crucified, a stumbling block to Jews and foolishness to Gentiles, but to those who are the called, both Jews and Greeks, Christ the power of God and the wisdom of God. For God's foolishness is wiser than human wisdom, and God's weakness is stronger than human strength.

The world demands success. Getting to the top, gaining fame and riches, being able to do it your way, these are the achievements which are daily presented to us as what life is all about. Though most of us have no chance of actually participating in that kind of success, we are encouraged to do so vicariously as we are called on to admire the 'personalities' of the age.

The world says, 'Blessed are the pushy, for they will get on in the world', but Jesus says, 'Blessed are the poor in spirit, for theirs is the kingdom of heaven.' The world says, 'Blessed are the thick-skinned, for they won't let anything hurt them', but Jesus says, 'Blessed are those who mourn, for they shall be comforted.' The world says, 'Blessed are those who assert themselves, for they will get their own way', but Jesus says, 'Blessed are the meek, for they will inherit the earth.' We could easily work our way through all the beatitudes (Matthew 5:3–12), seeing how they represent a complete reversal of the values which society naturally endorses.

The greatest reversal of all is represented by the crucified Messiah. The Jews, religious people who placed their hope in God's great act of vindication, were looking for a sign, an unambiguous demonstration of divine power and glory that would triumphantly fulfil the expectations of God's chosen people. The Greeks, intellectual people who felt that clear thinking would lead to the answers needed, were seeking wisdom. But God's wisdom turned out to be something entirely different—so much so that it looked like foolishness—just as God's power turned out to be something looking more like weakness in the world's eyes. God's wisdom was cruciform.

Does that mean that Christianity is a negative religion of masochism and failure? The great nineteenth-century critic of Christianity, Friedrich Nietzsche, contemptuously called it a religion for slaves. But the real slaves are those who are harnessed to the chariot of success in the illusive pursuit of becoming supermen and superwomen. Cruciform wisdom is realistic. It recognizes that this world is a vale of tears. It does not call on us to make crosses for ourselves. They will come to us through the limitations and disabilities from which no life can be free. Suffering is conquered, not by frantic flight, but by transcending acceptance. For to those who are called, both Jews and Greeks, the crucified Christ is the power of God and the wisdom of God.

PRAYER

Almighty God, whose most dear Son went not up to joy but first he suffered pain, and entered not into glory before he was crucified: mercifully grant that we, walking in the way of the cross, may find it none other than the way of life and peace; through Jesus Christ our Lord.

ASB, collect for Lent 3

Saturday

FREEDOM

I consider that the sufferings of this present time are not worth comparing with the glory about to be revealed to us. For the creation waits with eager longing for the revealing of the children of God; for the creation was subjected to futility, not of its own will but by the will of the one who subjected it, in hope that the creation itself will be set free from its bondage to decay and will obtain the freedom of the glory of the children of God.

We have been thinking how the necessary cost of an evolutionary world, making itself, lies in the raggedness and blind alleys of natural disasters. It is not only human experiences of suffering which are to be faced in the light of the cross. The whole of nature is cruciform. There is a clear sense in which St Paul is right when he says that the creation has been subjected to futility.

If that were the whole story, it would be a bleak story indeed. But in the mysterious but certain purposes of God, it is not the whole story. Death comes to all in this world, but there is a destiny beyond death. The whole creation will be set free from its bondage to decay and will obtain the freedom of the children of God.

I do not think that this world by itself makes sense. It is full of promise and fruitfulness, but if death and decay have the last word, then that promise and fruitfulness are transient and so, ultimately, illusory. We do not understand the sufferings of the present time aright unless we also are able to embrace the hope of a glory to be revealed to us.

Such a view has often been derided, as promising 'pie in the sky when you die'. If it was being suggested that present bitterness somehow didn't matter because of the heavenly treat that lay in store, I would agree that something unreal and unworthy was being proposed. But that is not the Christian understanding. Suffering is real, but it is not the only reality. Good Friday was not a charade or an irrelevancy for Jesus. It was an intense and dark experience, plumbing the depths of desolation. But Easter was equally real—not wiping out Good Friday as if it had never happened, but as showing that *through death* new life is given by God.

Nothing removes the tragedy of a young person dying from a dreadful congenital disease. But that tragedy is more intense, and indeed meaningless, if there is no sequel to it. The murderer really does triumph over his innocent victim if the latter's life is extinguished for ever. It is the ultimate and certain hope of freedom which redeems us from our present slavery to sin and death. Paul is very blunt about this. Writing to the Corinthians he says: 'If for this life only we have hoped in Christ, we are of all people most to be pitied... If with merely human hopes I fought with wild animals at Ephesus, what would I have gained by it? If the dead are not raised, "Let us eat and drink, for tomorrow we die"' (1 Corinthians 15:19, 32–33). It is God's purpose for the whole of his creation that it should attain freedom from its bondage to death.

PRAYER

Still let me prove thy perfect will,
My acts of faith and love repeat;
Till death thy endless mercies seal
And make the sacrifice complete.

Charles Wesley

THE WRONG QUESTION

Mark 11:1-10

When they were approaching Jerusalem, at Bethphage and Bethany, near the Mount of Olives, he sent two of his disciples and said to them, 'Go into the village ahead of you, and immediately as you enter it, you will find tied there a colt that has never been ridden; untie it and bring it. If anyone says to you, "Why are you doing this?" just say this, "The Lord needs it and will send it back here immediately."' They went away and found a colt tied near a door, outside in the street. As they were untying it, some of the bystanders said to them, 'What are you doing, untying the colt?' They told them what Jesus had said; and they allowed them to take it. Then they brought the colt to Jesus and threw their cloaks on it; and he sat on it. Many people spread their cloaks on the road, and others spread leafy branches that they had cut in the fields. Then those who went ahead and those who followed were shouting, 'Hosanna! Blessed is the one who comes in the name of the Lord! Blessed is the coming kingdom of our ancestor David! Hosanna in the highest heaven!'

The Passover was always a tricky time. Many of the pilgrims came a week early in order to go through the correct procedures of ritual cleansing before the actual celebration of the feast. The population of Jerusalem would be swollen to several times its normal size. The

Roman governor came up specially with his troops from his usual residence at Caesarea, in order to be able to keep an eye on things and to make sure they didn't get out of hand.

The crowds were excitable and volatile. In their minds was the great question, 'When is it going to happen?' They longed that God would vindicate his people, that the Romans would get their come-uppance and be expelled from Judea, that the kingdom of David would be restored, more glorious and powerful than ever before, that the Jewish people should shake the Gentile world. This year there seemed a possibility that it might actually happen. Jesus of Nazareth had been drawing the crowds. He was a charismatic figure. Could it be that he was the Messiah, the military conqueror who would lead the Jewish people out of subjection and into freedom, even domination?

No wonder there was a lot of excitement when Jesus actually rode into Jerusalem. The more reflective might have been given pause by the fact that he was riding a colt rather than a war horse, but for the crowd it was enough that he had come to the Holy City at this special time. They cried 'Hosanna!' ('Save now!'—let it happen) and risked trouble by showing their hopes of a victory to come, calling out, 'Blessed is the coming kingdom of our ancestor David!'

Because they had asked the wrong question, they were looking for the wrong answer. Jesus had not come to fight but to suffer. This week was to be the week of the passion. As its events unfold, the verbs used in the Gospel change their character. Up till now they have been active—Jesus is the one whose mighty words and deeds are being recounted; hereafter they change to the passive—Jesus is the one who is handed over to have things done to him.

Disappointment and dismay set in as it became clear that some wonderful deliverance was not on the cards but rather the power of the authorities would continue to prevail. It may well be that some of those who shouted 'Hosanna!' that first Palm Sunday were among the crowd that shouted 'Crucify him!' later in the week. Asking the wrong question, seeking the wrong answer, readily leads to disillusionment and bitterness.

PRAYER

God our Father, grant to us that we may seek first your kingdom and your righteousness, for the sake of him who died for us to fulfil your will.

HOLY WEEK

THE RIGHT QUESTION

Mark 11:27–33

Again [Jesus and the disciples] came to Jerusalem. As he was walking in the temple, the chief priests, the scribes, and the elders came to him and said, 'By what authority are you doing these things? Who gave you this authority to do them?' Jesus said to them, 'I will ask you one question; answer me, and I will tell you by what authority I do these things. Did the baptism of John come from heaven, or was it of human origin? Answer me.' They argued with one another, 'If we say, "From heaven," he will say, "Why then did you not believe him?" But shall we say, "Of human origin"?'—they were afraid of the crowd, for all regarded John as truly a prophet. So they answered Jesus, 'We do not know.' And Jesus said to them, 'Neither will I tell you by what authority I am doing these things.'

When you attempt to do scientific research, one of the hardest things is choosing the right question to try to answer. Is it a question to which an answer is in fact accessible in terms of present knowledge and technique? If so, is it a question which really gets to the heart of the matter, whose answer will illuminate what is going on? One of the things that one admires most about truly great scientists is their ability to ask the right questions, the ones that really matter.

One of the things I admire about Jesus is his ability to get straight to the point by asking exactly the right question. We see this happening in today's passage. The authorities come to him. They're upset by his apparently high-handed action in cleansing the temple. 'Who gave you the right to do that?' Jesus knows that they are unwilling to accept him as God's chosen representative. So, instead of answering them directly, he asks them a question in his turn, which will reveal just how closed their minds are to receiving a spiritual message. 'Who gave John the Baptist the authority for his special proclamation of repentance and the administration of baptism?' For the scribes and elders, snared in the web of their worldly calculations, that's a catch-22 question. If they say 'from God', then they stand convicted for not having responded to John; if they say 'from men', the people, who rightly perceive John to be a prophet, will be angry with them. As a result they can only mumble that they don't really know. By asking the right question, Jesus has shown clearly what was going on in the hearts of his opponents: their unwillingness to face the truth.

He does this all the time: healing on the sabbath (Mark 3:4); the tribute money (Mark 12:16); the nature of the Messiah (Mark 12:37). In these stories we see the record of an original and incisive mind at work, of one for whom the question of truth is paramount and who will cut through all obfuscation and pretence in order to get to it. Those of us who follow him and seek to serve the God of truth are called to be fearless and discerning in the questions that we ask, of others and of ourselves.

P R A Y E R

Lord open our minds to your truth and deliver us from the temptation to settle for half-truths and a facile avoidance of the real issues.

MORTALITY

Ecclesiastes 2:14–17

The wise have eyes in their head, but fools walk in darkness. Yet I perceived that the same fate befalls all of them. Then I said to myself, 'What happens to the fool will happen to me also; why then have I been so very wise?' And I said to myself that this also is vanity. For there is no enduring remembrance of the wise or of fools, seeing that in the days to come all will have been long forgotten. How can the wise die just like fools? So I hated life, because what is done under the sun was grievous to me; for all is vanity and a chasing after wind.

I once heard someone say in a sermon that finding the book Ecclesiastes bound up in the Bible gave you the same sort of shock that you would have if you saw a notorious atheist become a member of General Synod! The Preacher of Ecclesiastes has a pretty bleak view of the way things are. He is a king, rich, powerful, conventionally wise, but it all becomes dust and ashes—vanity!—for him when he contemplates the fact of human mortality. As Shakespeare put it, 'Golden lads and lasses must, as chimney sweepers, come to dust.' Death is the great leveller and in the end the grave is the destiny of us all.

So what is the Preacher up to? How did he sneak into scripture? Certainly one of the reasons he is there is to remind us that facts are facts. In his sober way, he looks with an unblinking eye on the human condition. We are all going to die, even if we are a famous pop star or have just won the national lottery.

It is a commonplace to say that death has replaced sex as the great taboo topic in our society. It is hushed up and tidied out of the way. But we shall only be free to live life if we are also free to acknowledge that it is leading us to our death. We may feel that it was somewhat morbidly ridiculous for someone like John Donne to dress himself in a shroud and sleep in his coffin, as a preparation for the act of dying. Yet it is fecklessly foolish to live as if we are immortal.

This week is all about a death. The agony of Gethsemane and the darkness of Calvary make it clear that death was a reality for Jesus, as it will be for us. There is no pretence in the Bible that death is somehow not a real end. But it is not the ultimate end. Only God is ultimate and Easter shows us that reality is not terminated by death.

I regularly pray that I may be given grace to die a good death when my time comes. By that I do not mean simply that I may be spared great pain and suffering, though naturally I hope that may be so. What I really hope for above all is that I may be able to accept my dying and to see that it is my final act in this life of committing myself, fully and hopefully, into the hands of my heavenly Father.

P R A Y E R

Lord, may we so learn to trust you in life, that we
may also come to trust you wholly in death as we
commit ourselves into the hands of a merciful
Creator and faithful Redeemer.

THE FAITHFULNESS OF GOD

Mark 12:24–27

Jesus said to [the Sadducees], 'Is not this the reason you are wrong, that you know neither the scriptures nor the power of God? For when they rise from the dead, they neither marry nor are given in marriage, but are like angels in heaven. And as for the dead being raised, have you not read in the book of Moses, in the story about the bush, how God said to him, 'I am the God of Abraham, the God of Isaac, and the God of Jacob'? He is God not of the dead, but of the living; you are quite wrong.'

In today's story we have another instance of Jesus' incisive mind at work, getting to the very heart of the matter.

A party of Sadducees had come to talk with him, hoping to catch him out. They were the ruling Jewish party in Jerusalem and they were very conservative in their beliefs. Only the Torah, the five books of Moses, Genesis to Deuteronomy, were good enough for them as scripture. They did not feel they found there any indication that there was a human destiny beyond death. Accordingly they believed in a life in this world only.

The Sadducees thought they could make their point to Jesus in a rather clever way, by presenting him with a puzzle. Jewish respect for the continuance of the family required that if a married man died childless his brother should marry the widow in order to raise children in the dead man's memory. The Sadducees propounded the case of a woman and seven brothers, all of whom died childless, and to all of whom she had been married in turn. If there is a life to come, whose wife would she be then? In other words, how do the entanglements and incomplete relationships of this world find their resolution and completion in the next?

There is a rabbinical tradition of Jewish thinking which delights in the search for understanding through the exploration of knotty problems of this kind, but Jesus will have none of it. He goes to the basic issue and uses Exodus, one of the books the Sadducees accepted, to make his point. God told Moses that he was the God of the patriarchs, Abraham, Isaac and Jacob. Think what that must mean, Jesus says. When Abraham died, God had not finished with him, discarding him as one might throw away a broken pot which was no longer any use. Because Abraham had mattered to God once, he must matter to him for ever. 'He is God not of the dead, but of the living.'

The fundamental reason why we may hope with confidence for a destiny beyond our death is that God is faithful. His steadfast love will never let us go. That was good enough for Jesus. It should have been good enough for the Sadducees. It is good enough for us.

As we think of Jesus' words, we should remember that they were not spoken just as part of an academic discussion but at the very time he knew that the authorities were seeking to kill him and in the very week in which he submitted himself to painful death.

P R A Y E R

Lord God, faithful and merciful, we trust you in life and in death, for ourselves and for those we love, for you are the God, not of the dead, but of the living.

DO THIS

1 Corinthians 11:23-26

*For I received from the Lord what I also handed on to
you, that the Lord Jesus on the night when he was
betrayed took a loaf of bread, and when he had given
thanks, he broke it and said, 'This is my body that is for
you. Do this in remembrance of me.' In the same way he
took the cup also, after supper, saying, 'This cup is the
new covenant in my blood. Do this, as often as you drink
it, in remembrance of me.' For as often as you eat this
bread and drink the cup, you proclaim the Lord's death
until he comes.*

All the Gospels contain a description of the last meal that
Jesus shared with his disciples. Matthew, Mark and Luke
speak of Jesus' words over the bread and the cup of wine.
John gives what is clearly his eucharistic teaching in a
different form (John 6:35–59). However, the earliest
account we have of the Lord's supper is that which Paul
called to the remembrance of his Corinthian
converts—what he had received from the Lord and had
handed on to them.

Jesus' reference to his body and blood must have
seemed very strange to his first hearers. Because it was
forbidden in the Law, Jewish people had an abhorrence of
the idea of drinking blood. These shocking words were
being used to convey in a vivid, unforgettable way the gift
of life being made to those who followed the command to

'Do this'. It is a sad irony, that the later history of the Christian Church has been so marred by bitter disputes about what exactly is the manner of the Lord's presence in the eucharist. One of the wisest responses was made by Queen Elizabeth I at a time when such controversies were raging very fiercely. Asked for her opinion about Christ's presence in the sacrament, she said

> 'Twas God the word who spake it,
> He took the bread and brake it;
> And what the word did make it;
> That I believe and take it.

There are two important things to be said. One is that throughout the centuries, Christians have found in the sacrament of the holy communion a source of life and strength and a place of meeting with the presence of their risen Lord. There have been a variety of theories of the Mass, but one experience.

The other thing to say is to remind ourselves that when we gather round the Lord's table, we do so fulfilling his command to us to 'Do this in remembrance of him'. An Anglican Benedictine monk, Dom Gregory Dix, wrote:

> Was ever another command so obeyed? For century after century, spreading slowly to every continent and country and among every race on earth, this action has been done, in every conceivable human need from infancy and before it to extreme old age and after it, from the pinnacles of earthly greatness to the refuge of fugitives in the caves and dens of the earth... week by week and month by month, on a hundred successive Sundays, faithfully, unfailingly, across all the parishes of christendom, the pastors have done just this to make the plebs sancta Dei—the holy common people of God

> The Shape of the Liturgy, *page 744*

PRAYER

As watchmen look for the morning, so we look for you, O Christ. Come to us and make yourself known in the breaking of the bread; for you are our God for ever and ever.

DARKNESS

Mark 15:33–34

When it was noon, darkness came over the whole land until three in the afternoon. At three o'clock Jesus cried out with a loud voice, 'Eloi, Eloi, lema sabachthani?' which means, 'My God, my God, why have you forsaken me?'

The deepest darkness of Calvary is the spiritual darkness out of which comes the terrible cry, 'My God, my God, why have you forsaken me?' It says something for the honesty of the Gospel writers that Matthew and Mark both record the cry of dereliction.

It is Jesus who utters this cry—Jesus, the one who throughout his life had trusted absolutely in the care of his heavenly Father, who even in the dismay of Gethsemane used the intimate word 'Abba' in his prayer to God. In the desolation of these hours of deep darkness, such familiar language is no longer possible, it seems. Yet it is still God who is addressed by Jesus. In the most profound suffering, he never lets go of God. As he hangs on the cross, Jesus holds on—just—to the One who has been the centre of his life.

What is going on in this intense and sombre scene? We are taken back again to the words of Gregory of Nazianzus: 'What is not assumed is not healed.' Jesus came to share fully in human experience, so that all that experience might be healed and redeemed. Everything must be shared, even the ultimate desolation of the experience of God-forsakenness. Indeed, perhaps most of all that dereliction, for without its redemption human despair cannot be turned into human hope. St Paul put it with startling clarity: 'For our sake God made him to be sin who knew no sin, so that in him we might become the righteousness of God' (2 Corinthians 5:21). That is the mysterious transaction of the darkness of the cross.

Remember, that in Christian understanding, it is God himself who stands on both sides of that transaction. The paradox of Calvary is that it is God, living the life of a man, who submits himself to the human experience of God-forsakeness. Words give out at this point. All we can do is to be still and thankful, in silent awe at the mystery of our redemption.

P R A Y E R

*Today he who hung the earth upon the waters
is hung upon the Cross.
He who is King of the angels
is arrayed in a crown of thorns.
He who wraps the heaven in clouds
is wrapped in purple mockery.
The Bridegroom of the Church
is transfixed with nails.
The eternal Son of the Father crys
'My God, my God why have you forsaken me?'
We venerate your passion, O Christ.*

Orthodox Good Friday hymn, adapted

JOSEPH OF ARIMATHEA

Mark 15:42–47

*When the evening had come, and since it was the day of
Preparation, that is, the day before the sabbath, Joseph of
Arimathea, a respected member of the council, who was
also himself waiting expectantly for the kingdom of God,
went boldly to Pilate and asked for the body of Jesus.
Then Pilate wondered if he were already dead; and
summoning the centurion, he asked him whether he had
been dead for some time. When he learned from the
centurion that he was dead, he granted the body to
Joseph. Then Joseph bought a linen cloth, and taking
down the body, wrapped it in the linen cloth, and laid it
in a tomb that had been hewn out of the rock. He then
rolled a stone against the door of the tomb. Mary
Magdalene and Mary the mother of Joses saw where the
body was laid.*

It was the Roman custom to cast the dead bodies of
condemned felons into a common and anonymous grave.
There was one man who was determined that this should
not happen to Jesus. His name was Joseph and he came
from the small Jewish town of Arimathea. All we know
about him is what we can read in this passage. One of the
reasons for believing the story to be true is precisely that an
undistinguished person, of no known subsequent significance in the Christian Church, is given the honourable
action of burying the Lord's body. The only plausible

reason for assigning this important role to Joseph is that he actually performed it.

It required some courage. Joseph was a man of standing in the community, 'a respected member of the council'. Matthew tells us that he was rich (Matthew 27:57). We do not know what role he had played in the preceding events of Jesus' trial and handing over for execution. It seems likely that he had kept his head down and avoided trouble. Yet he was 'waiting expectantly for the kingdom of God' and, although the events of Good Friday might have seemed to signal the dashing of such hopes, Joseph decided that there was one final gesture that was worth making. At the risk of ridicule or rejection, he went to Pilate to ask for Jesus' corpse. The governor was surprised that he was already dead: after all, the point of crucifixion was not to make death quick. But Jesus had undergone spiritual suffering of a kind that was far beyond Pilate's power to imagine. Since it turned out that 'the King of the Jews' had expired so rapidly, Pilate was content to let Joseph have his way. The man from Arimathea quickly removed the body, anxious to complete the business before the sabbath began at sundown. Fortunately he had a new tomb of his own, all ready nearby, and that was where he laid the dead Jesus.

Jesus had some strange companions and supporters in the hours of his death and passion: two thieves, one of whom placed his hope in Christ when all things seemed past hope; and a hard-bitten Roman NCO who was was moved to exclaim 'Truly this man was God's Son!' (Mark 15:39). Perhaps the strangest of all was this well-to-do Jewish councillor, moved at the last to do a decent thing and thereby winning for himself perpetual remembrance and a privilege beyond his wildest imagining. We none of us know what may be the significance of our small kindnesses and faithful gestures.

*P*RAYER

Almighty God, your most dear Son Jesus Christ lay this day in the tomb in obedience to your will. May we, by your grace, be buried with him to die to sin so that we may rise with him to everlasting life.

THE EMPTY TOMB

Luke 24:1–5

*But on the first day of the week, at early dawn, they came
to the tomb, taking the spices that they had prepared.
They found the stone rolled away from the tomb, but
when they went in, they did not find the body. While they
were perplexed about this, suddenly two men in dazzling
clothes stood beside them. The women were terrified and
bowed their faces to the ground, but the men said to
them, 'Why do you look for the living among the dead?
He is not here, but has risen.'*

Nowhere in the New Testament is there a description of
the resurrection itself. That mighty act of God was unseen
and it is indescribable. When the women reach the tomb,
the resurrection has already taken place. What they find is
the sepulchre empty and the stone rolled away. Their first
reaction is not joy but perplexity. They have come to pay
their last respects and they do not know what to make of
this. They fear that the body of Jesus has been stolen in an
act of desecration.

No one was expecting Jesus to rise from the dead. Many
Jews believed in a general resurrection at the end of
history but no one expected a particular resurrection
within history. Notice that we are talking of resurrection
(someone coming alive never to die again), not a resuscita-
tion (the revival of someone who would certainly die later).
Belief in the resurrection was assuredly not the product of

wishful expectation. The empty tomb was a puzzle needing explanation.

In Luke's version of the story, the interpretation of what had happened is given by the two angelic men in dazzling clothes. 'Why do you look for the living among the dead? He is not here, but has risen.'

The logic of the resurrection is the triumph of life over death. God is the God, not of the dead, but of the living. Therefore his Christ must be found, not among the dead, but among the living. The last word lies always with God and life. The resurrection of Jesus is a triple vindication.

First, it is the vindication of Jesus himself. It was not fitting that his life of love should end in failure, that death and dereliction should vanquish life and faithfulness.

Secondly, it is the vindication of God. Despite the appearances on that first Good Friday, God did not abandon the one man who wholly trusted himself to him, but stood by him in death and beyond death. God proved himself indeed to be the God of the living.

Thirdly, it is the vindication of human hopes, the intuition deep in our hearts that life has a meaning and fulfilment which death will not be allowed to frustrate, the truth of the assurance that came to Julian of Norwich that in the end all shall be well and all manner of things shall be well.

No wonder that Easter is the most joyful day of all the year.

'This is the day that the Lord has made; let us rejoice and be glad in it' (Psalm 118:24).

The One whom the tomb could not contain says to us, as he said to John on Patmos, 'Do not be afraid; I am the first and the last, and the living one. I was dead, and see, I am alive for ever and ever; and I have the keys of Death and Hades' (Revelation 1:17–18). Alleluia! Jesus lives!

PRAYER

Love's redeeming work is done;
Fought the fight, the battle won:
Lo, our Sun's eclipse is o'er!
Lo, he sets in blood no more.
Lives again our glorious King;
Where, O death, is now thy sting?
Dying once, he all doth save;
Where thy victory, O grave?

Charles Wesley